THE HERTFORDSHIRE
COOK BOOK

A CELEBRATION OF THE AMAZING FOOD & DRINK ON OUR DOORSTEP

The Hertfordshire Cook Book

©2020 Meze Publishing Ltd. All rights reserved.

First edition printed in 2020 in the UK.

ISBN: 978-1-910863-64-0

Compiled by: Becky Alexander, Anna Tebble

Written by: Becky Alexander

Photography by: Paul Gregory

Edited by: Katie Fisher, Phil Turner

Designed by: Paul Cocker

Contributors: Michael Johnson, Sarah Koriba, Paul Stimpson

Cover art: Luke Prest (www.lukeprest.com)

Printed by Bell and Bain Ltd, Glasgow

Published by Meze Publishing Limited
Unit 1b, 2 Kelham Square
Kelham Riverside
Sheffield S3 8SD
Web: www.mezepublishing.co.uk
Telephone: 0114 275 7709
Email: info@mezepublishing.co.uk

CONTENTS

WELCOME TO HERTFORDSHIRE

FOOD COLUMNIST FOR *THE HERTS ADVERTISER* AND AUTHOR BECKY ALEXANDER, WELCOMES YOU TO EXPERIENCE THE DELICIOUS FOOD AND DRINK TO BE FOUND IN HERTFORDSHIRE: THE 'COUNTY OF OPPORTUNITY'.

Did you know that Hertfordshire is the home of the original hot cross bun? And the oldest pub in the UK? We also have a baker who supplies scones to Wimbledon each year, as well as our very own chocolate factory. Hertfordshire is also home to the best martini in the world! Close to London and all of the new food trends, but also rural enough to grow food, Hertfordshire has a thriving, vibrant food and drink scene, as anyone who lives here will already know.

With busy market towns, cities and villages, there really is something for everyone, from street food to farmers' markets. We have a long history of brewing in the county; McMullens opened in Hertford in 1827 and has many pubs in the area, but we also have newcomers such as Farr Brew. Ye Olde Fighting Cocks dates back to the 11th century, and has a long history of brewing for the Abbey (now St Albans Cathedral). The monks at the Cathedral are responsible for the original hot cross bun, known as the Alban bun, which dates back to the 14th century. You can buy them in the Cathedral café in the run up to Easter each year; you will see that the cross isn't piped like many commercial buns but is cut into the dough. Simmons has been baking in Hatfield since 1838 and has grown across Hertfordshire, with most towns and villages having at least one shop. They have a long history of baking thousands of scones for Wimbledon! If puds are more your thing, then head to The Pudding Stop for amazing puds by former Bake Off contestant Johnny Shepherd. The puds are so good they now also sell in Selfridges. Campfire Gin is made over at Puddingstone Distillery (puddingstone is a stone unique to Hertfordshire) and is the main ingredient in Ben's martini which was crowned winner in the World's Best Martini Challenge in 2019.

As you explore the county you will see many farms and farm shops, and the quality of fresh vegetables and meats is outstanding. Pearces are known across the county for their own berries, vegetables and high-welfare meats and Glinwells grow the most delicious tomatoes, peppers and aubergines, to give you just a small taste. Many of our indies collaborate and you will often see local products in the delis and farm shops or being used by each other; Dizzy Bee Granola, for example, uses Chiltern Oils award-winning rapeseed oil in their recipes. There is so much to discover, old favourites and new, and I hope you enjoy reading about some of my favourites collected here!

THE FAMILY FARM SHOP

FOR 60 YEARS BATTLERS GREEN FARM HAS CATERED FOR THE RADLETT COMMUNITY, AND NOW PEOPLE FROM ALL OVER HERTFORDSHIRE FLOCK TO THEIR FARM SHOP AND DELI FOR DELICIOUS FOOD.

In a lovely farmyard setting on the outskirts of Radlett you'll find Battlers Green Farm Shop, a treasure-trove of useful and delicious foods. The farm 'shop' started in 1960 when Joan Haworth began selling eggs, milk and cream from the back door to the nearby village residents to supplement the family's income. Now, 60 years later, the stylish shop, managed by mum Gillian, is home to a great deli counter, shelves packed with larder essentials, breads and bakes, dairy products, wine, gin and beer, the Cook range of meals, and much more!

The cheese counter is a big draw for local customers and has an impressive range of British and continental cheeses, along with crackers and chutneys. One of the bestsellers in the shop is the cottage cheese from Longley Farm in Holmfirth, and Andrew Haworth (Joan's grandson) says it is amazing and the best in the UK. Smoked ham, salami and other cold cuts, along with sausage rolls, pies and scotch eggs fill the cold meats counter, and you can select deli olives, stuffed peppers and other antipasti treats by the potful.

Baskets of bread from Herts-based Simmons Bakery fill one wall, and their loaves, rolls and cakes are always popular. Bury Lane Bakery in Royston and Farmhouse Cookery provide many of the cakes and biscuits, and the shop also sells one

of the best ranges of gluten-free bakes in the county; Lynn Elliot from Mellyn Bakes, Welwyn Garden City produces the quiches, cakes and pies, all wheat-free.

Every day larder stockers including pastas, pulses and baking goods line the nearby shelves, along with preserves and sauces. Honey comes from nearby Aldenham and The Wooden Spoon Preserving Company supply many of the jams and marmalades.

A large room along from the deli is stocked with Cook meals, which are hugely popular; you can pick up a vegetarian, fish or meat-based main course from one to twelve servings, including Moroccan tagines, fish pies and chicken curries. The farm shop also has a great selection of wines, beers and spirits including many from local companies including Campfire, The 3 Brewers and Tring Brewery.

If you have time, pop into the family-owned The Bull Pen café across the courtyard (the building dates to the early 1900s). You will also spot Brimarks Butchers (they sell the farm's Aberdeen Angus beef), Weston's Fishmongers, Reed's Fruiterers, and Spiceway; it is a foodie destination that brings in people from all over Hertfordshire and beyond!

GILLIAN'S MEAN GREEN CANAPÉS

A delightfully mouth-watering, quick and easy vegetarian canapé! This uses some of the lovely products we sell in the shop, such as Longley Farm cream cheese, which is truly delicious.

FOR THE PANCAKES

120g plain flour

2 large eggs

300ml milk

Pinch of salt

1 tbsp sunflower or vegetable oil, plus a little extra for frying

FOR THE CANAPÉS

Longley Farm Cream Cheese (roughly 100g per pancake, depending on the size)

Mr Cori Chilli's Cori Chilli (roughly 100g per pancake, depending on the size)

FOR THE PANCAKES

Mix the flour, eggs, milk, salt and a tablespoon of vegetable oil until smooth and leave to stand for 30 minutes.

Grease a shallow frying pan with vegetable oil. Ladle a spoonful of batter into the pan over a medium heat. Swirl the batter around the pan to cover the base. Cook for around 1 minute on each side until lightly browned.

Transfer the pancakes to a warmed plate and cover to keep warm.

FOR THE CANAPÉS

Spread a layer of cream cheese on to a pancake. Spread a layer of Cori Chilli over the cream cheese.

Roll the pancake into a long sausage shape. Trim off the ends for neatness, then cut into bite-size portions around 1 inch wide. Arrange on a plate, ready to serve!

ALTERNATIVES

You could substitute Cori Chilli for Wooden Spoon's Onion Marmalade or The Garlic Farm's Garlic Jam.

Preparation time: 40 minutes | Cooking time: 10 minutes | Makes around 60 canapés

JOIN THE CULT

LIMITED-EDITION CRAFT BEERS SIT ALONGSIDE THE VERY BEST INTERNATIONAL ALES, AND LOCALS POP IN FOR A DRINK AT THE END OF A BUSY DAY AT BEER SHOP IN ST ALBANS AND HITCHIN.

John and Ben started Beer Shop before they even had a shop. Starting out at farmers' markets and touring festivals in Hertfordshire and North London in their VW campervan, they wanted to find out if there was interest in the indie, limited edition beers that they loved. Happily, there was, and they now run two bottle shop and tasting rooms, where people who want to try something new head to find "fuss beers" that they can't find in larger outlets.

Being small and independent themselves mean that they can react quickly when a new beer is released. As John explains, "it's a bit like getting Glastonbury tickets; you have to be quick else they're gone!" If you want Cloudwater, Verdant, Pressure Drop and other limited editions, head to the laid-back boutique shops in Hitchin and St Albans. If you are not sure what you like, they have a small selection of cask and keg beers on tap that you can drink by the glass, either a third, half or two-thirds of a pint. It's a great way to try something new, without over-committing, and if you love it, you can fill a container to take home.

Shelves and fridges line the walls of both shops and are filled with brightly coloured bottles and cans, many of which are modern, hoppy IPAs and pale ales that are so popular now. Sour and wild beers, made with wild yeasts and aged in barrels are a new trend, and worth trying. You can taste the terroir, their relationship with the flora and fauna of the environment where the beer is fermented and barrel-aged; one for enthusiasts of complex, interesting beers. John and Ben also like to support local suppliers, and they stock a range of Hertfordshire indies including Tring, The 3 Brewers and Pope's Yard Brewery.

Brewing has always been at the heart of what they do, so it was a natural step to start Bubble Works Brew Co. Ben tends to do most of the brewing over in Hitchin, and every couple of weeks Bubble Works release a limited edition beer that sells on tap in both shops. The only make 100 litres at a time, so you do need to get in quick. "We know what we love and what our customers love – juicy, New England-style Pales and IPAs," say the duo, who enjoy experimenting and perfecting recipes.

We've created a step-by-step tasting session with a selection of styles and beers that we usually keep in stock at Beer Shop. Due to the bottle sizes it's best to enjoy this tasting session with two or more friends. There's a glass for every beer style (some might say) but to keep it simple we recommend using a tulip-shaped glass to capture the aroma; a large wine glass would work perfectly. Swirl the glass a little but not too much or the beers will go flat. Take a sniff first. Then taste; remember that unlike wine, beer must be swallowed; this is because bitterness is integral, and that can only be detected at the back of your tongue.

STYLE 1: HEFEWEIZEN

A great place to start a tasting session; they're light, pillowy beers with heaps of character due to their unmistakable yeast (hefe) which produces distinctive notes of banana and clove.

Beer: Ayinger Urweisse 5.8% ABV

Region: Bavaria, Germany

Tasting notes: Strong head retention with banana and clove aromas. A fruity-tart body with hints of orange and banoffee flavours.

Food pairing: Try pairing these with seafood salads like asparagus and crab, or maybe vegetable sushi and wasabi.

Also try: Andechser Weissbier Hell

STYLE 2: PALE ALE

The most popular style category by far with a multitude of subcategories, however it typically consists of clean pale malts backed up by hop bitterness. Modern pales use new world hops with bold fruity aromas while traditional English pales or Belgian pales are more bitter, herbal and earthy.

beer: The Kernel Brewery Pale Ale 5.4% ABV

Region: London, England

Tasting notes: A simple malt base gives way allowing the hop aromas to shine. Rotating hops in every batch means you'll get something new every time, so they're the perfect way to learn what you prefer.

Food pairing: Bready pale malts work with pizza, pasta and burger dishes while hops cut through the grease. When bitter, earthy or fruity hop flavours dominate, complement with spices and hot sauces.

Also try: Orval by Brasserie d'Orval

STYLE 3: SMOKED/TOASTED

Malt can be smoked during the kilning (drying) process and is used in 'smoked' beers. Malts are also kilned to varying grades providing more robust toasty flavours, for example in German Doppelbocks or traditional English Porters.

Beer: Aecht Schlenkerla Rauchbier Märzen 5.1% ABV

Region: Bamberg, Germany

Tasting notes: Brewed with Original Schlenkerla Smokemalt from the brewery's in-house maltings. A strong and distinctive aroma of smoked bacon and spicy cured meats. A velvety mouthfeel and similar taste as aroma, plus a slight bitterness with a lingering smoky finish.

Food pairing: These beers pair with hearty main courses like chilli con carne and grilled foods like bratwurst or kebabs.

Also try: The Chiltern Brewery Lord-Lieutenant's Cream Porter

STYLE 4: 'SLOW' SOUR BEER

They deserve a tasting session of their own due to their diversity. Acidity drives the flavour profile but you can expect vinous-like qualities, tannins from the barrels they're aged in, floral and stone fruit aromas and varying degrees of funk.

Beer: Brouwerij Rodenbach Grand Cru 6% ABV

Region: Roeselare, Belgium

Tasting notes: Oak aged, fruity, complex and intense aroma. Upfront acid sourness, red berry fruit, oak and caramel to finish.

Food pairing: We'd recommend having some stinky cheeses or cured meats with this one.

Also try: 3 Fonteinen Oude Geuze

STYLE 5: NEW ENGLAND IPA

Juicy, hazy and intensely hoppy with low bitterness. Yeast strains provide stone fruit-like esters and hops are chosen for dank, tropical and citrus profiles.

Beer: Verdant - any IPA or DIPA 6.5 - 8% ABV

Region: Cornwall, England

Tasting notes: Recipes vary from week to week but their IPAs and DIPAs are some of the best juicy, hazy and hoppy bangers currently produced in the UK. Hops and yeast are used together to create cocktails of dank and juicy fruit flavours.

Food pairing: If you've still space for food try a mango or pineapple salsa with tortilla, white meats or fish.

Also try: Cloudwater, any IPA or DIPA

THE HOLY TRINITY

CHEESE, WINE AND CRAFT BEER: WHAT'S NOT TO LOVE?

The Bishop's Cave is the brainchild of Dan and Steve (son and father) who decided to open their hybrid craft beer, wine and cheese bar and shop while discussing their future aspirations during a round of golf. Named after the town, the first Bishop's Cave opened in Bishop's Stortford on North Street in 2015.

The idea is that you can pop in and buy a bottle of wine or beer and some cheese to takeaway, or grab a chair around one of the many tables and drink and eat in while soaking up the atmosphere.

You can stay for a quick beer, or glass of wine, or book a table with friends and make a night of it. "We wanted to create a relaxed, continental-style bar where people can come and enjoy some of life's little luxuries," explains Dan.

They take craft beer seriously, and there is a great range of cans, from the UK and beyond, to choose from as well as four rotating beers on draft.

Their wine selection is amazing, with something for every taste; Argentinian Malbec is popular, as is Gamay and Merlot from France. For a very special occasion you might choose the Santenay Premier Cru from 1998 or something off-menu from the private cellar. It is a chance to try something you wouldn't usually go for (and they hold regular tasting sessions so that you can taste many of them). They also offer the option of buying high quality wine by the glass

A glass of dessert wine with your cheese is perfect if you are going to the Cave after dinner elsewhere; you could order a cheeseboard to share along with a glass of Messias LBV 2013 or Coteaux de Layon Premier Cru. There are sparkling wines available from around the world, and it's great to see some local wine on the list too. They are currently serving the Bacchus and Hudshill Dry from Essex winemaker Hazel End.

The cheese is displayed in a large counter, and you can make up your own cheeseboard, which they serve with plenty of crackers, chutney and grapes. Charcuterie boards, paté, antipasti, pork pies and huge scotch eggs are available too! Not to mention the chocolate pairings for the end of the evening.

In 2017, the second bar opened in St Albans, within the Cathedral Quarter on Holywell Hill. It is a cosy yet funky space, with exposed brickwork, beams and tiled flooring showcasing the beautiful 600-year-old building. The latest addition is The Gin Cave next door on Holywell Hill, where they have an astonishing range of over 80 small batch gins, expertly matched with a variety of different mixers and cocktail combinations. As they say, 'If you don't like gin, you just haven't found the right one yet!' The gin menu is arranged by key flavor profiles such as "Juniper and Forthright" and "Floral and Fruity" to help you choose. They also have non-gin-based cocktails like the Nectar of Death, a spiced rum twist on an Old Fashioned, or the popular wine-based Bishop's Spritz. Cheers!

THE BISHOP'S CAVE
CHEESE & WINE LOVERS' GUIDE

*Cheese and wine together is one of life's pleasures, so here is our guide to
matching them to make the most of the different textures and flavours. There are
so many amazing cheeses and wines to experience, so why not try something new?*

SOFT GOAT'S CHEESE AND SPARKLING ROSÉ

The slight acidity and fruitiness of the sparkling rosé works
perfectly with the texture and flavour of the soft goat's
cheese.

We suggest: A Fivemiletown Boilie log with South
African Simonsig Kaapse Vonkel MCC Rosé, which is a
unique sparkling rosé using Pinotage and Pinot Noir grapes.
Fivemiletown Creamery is based in County Tyrone in
Northern Ireland.

STRONG BLUE AND CABERNET FRANC

The fruitiness and full body of a Cabernet Franc perfectly
matches the power and full flavour of the blue cheese.
Cabernet Franc or wines with firm tannins are particularly
good with goat's or sheep's milk blue cheeses which carry
that little extra punch.

We suggest: Valdeon with the Garage Wine Co. Cabernet
Franc. Valdeon is made in the mountains of Picos de Europa
and also pairs well with our Walnut and Honey crackers.

HARD SHEEP'S CHEESE AND MALBEC

Rich and full-bodied wines such as Malbec will pair perfectly
with salty, buttery, hard cheeses such as Manchego or
Mahon. The richness of the wine as well as firm but well-
integrated tannins balances the saltiness of strong, well-aged
cheeses.

We suggest: Mahon with El Enemigo Malbec. Our Mahon
is a cheese native to Menorca and is aged while being washed
in olive oil, paprika and tomato pulp.

BRIE-STYLE CHEESE AND SAUVIGNON BLANC

Traditionally, one might pair a brie with a Champagne or
similar sparkling wine. While this works, when the cheese is
wonderfully ripe and has added strength, the sharp grapefruit
flavours present in a Sauvignon Blanc create a better overall
balance.

We suggest:
Baron Bigod with Two Rivers Sauvignon Blanc. Baron Bigod
is an English Brie from the Fen Farm dairy in Suffolk. Try their
truffled version around Christmas time for a real treat.

WASHED RIND CHEESE AND DESSERT WINE

With a washed rind cheese, there is added pungency,
especially when the cheese has been washed in alcohol, such
as Stinking Bishop or Epoisses. We think the best partner for
that is something sweet, but light, with a little acidity like a
Tokaji or Coteaux de Layon.

We suggest: Epoisses with Coteaux De Layon Premier
Cru. Epoisses is a classic French cheese from the Bourgogne
region that is hand brushed in brandy while it matures.

CHEDDAR AND MERLOT

Cheddar comes in all shapes and sizes but the best ones
tend to be subtle as well as salty. So as not to lose the
amazing subtleties of a traditional unpasteurised cheddar-like
Pitchfork or Westcombe, a Merlot-driven wine will work
well given the slightly lighter body. Right bank Bordeaux is
particularly good as their Merlot is more softly structured
and elegant than their new world counterparts.

We suggest: Pitchfork with Chateau Vieux Bonneau
Montagne St Emilion. Pitchfork, from Trethowan's Dairy in
Somerset, was awarded the title of 'Best British Cheese' at
the World Cheese Awards in 2019.

SWISS CHEESE AND PINOT NOIR

The creaminess of Swiss hard cheese and the slightly more
nuanced, lower salt content varieties in particular call for a
lower acidity, light to medium-bodied wine. Pinot Noir fits
this bill perfectly. Fruity red Burgundy is our choice as the
smooth tannin and bright red fruit will harmoniously sit with
the Swiss cheese.

We suggest: Starnachas with Chateau de Santenay
Mercurey Premier cru. Starnachas, voted 'World's Best
Cheese' in 2016 is made by Affineur Walo and is aged
for 8 months and sits somewhere between Gruyère and
Appenzeller.

ITALIAN FOOD?
IT'S ALL HERE!

BUONGIORNO ITALIA IS A FRIENDLY, HELPFUL DELI PACKED FULL OF DELICIOUS ITALIAN FOODS, FRESH VEGETABLES AND FRUITS, CHEESE, CHARCUTERIE, ANTIPASTI, FINE WINES AND MUCH, MUCH MORE...

"Ladies and Gentlemen, welcome to Buongiorno Italia, Italy on your doorstep right here in the wonderful city of St Albans!" says Tony, the owner of the vibrant, award-winning deli established in 1978 by his parents.

Customers, many known by name, are always made to feel welcome and part of the family, whether they are in the store to buy a delicious filled ciabatta and coffee for a takeaway lunch, a quick easy meal for tonight's dinner, or a selection of meat, cheese and antipasti for that special occasion with guests.

If you love Italian food, live in Hertfordshire and haven't yet discovered Buongiorno Italia you must make a trip. Shelves are bursting with a huge selection of useful, time-saving, authentic groceries and hard-to-get good quality, full of flavour ingredients that will make a huge difference to your Italian meals.

One of the best deli counters in the south east of England, Buongiorno Italia is packed with Italian fresh sausages, salami, arancini, homemade lasagne, olives, antipasto, filled fresh pasta, and great selection of over 35 cheeses.

Everything you need is right here, from true Italian mortadella, fiery ndjua and gianciale to creamy buffalo milk burrata and mozzarella, gorgonzola, taleggio, pecorino and parmiggiano. Juicy olives, marinated Sicilian artichokes, filled sweet peppers, mixed seafood salad and a great range of fresh pestos. The frozen pizza dough is a bestseller and the team can help you pick out ingredients for easy toppings, and why not pick up some Sicilian canolis too. Along with fresh bread, selected fruit and vegetables and some great wine, Buongiorno Italia is truly a fully stocked, one-stop Italian food shop.

At Christmas the shop is overflowing with seasonal products such as panforte, nougat and pistachio paste. It also boasts one of the best selection of Panettone of different flavours and fillings as well as the classic and traditional that just keeps clients returning year after year.

This Italian deli is a gem… staying true to its 40-year heritage, moving forward with food trends and where the customer care is the heart and soul of its popularity. Make the trip!

We've chosen three great pasta dishes using our favourite, bestselling, quick and easy to use products.

PESTO AND ROASTED VEGETABLE LINGUINE

200g Seggiano basil pesto

500g La Molisana no.7 Mezze Linguine

1 red pepper, deseeded, cored and chopped

1 yellow pepper, deseeded, cored and chopped

1 red onion, peeled and finely chopped

300g cherry tomatoes, halved

1 large clove of garlic, peeled and finely sliced

1 tbsp Basso extra-virgin olive oil

Olives, optional

Parmesan, to serve

Preheat the oven to 200°c. Place the vegetables in a roasting tin. Toss in the olive oil and roast in the oven for approximately 20 minutes or until cooked and slightly charred.

Meanwhile, cook the pasta according to the instructions. When ready, drain well.

Add the pasta to the tray of vegetables with the pesto and mix well. Add olives to the dish if desired. Serve with shavings of parmesan.

SICILIAN CHERRY TOMATO SAUCE WITH PANCETTA AND PEA PENNE

140g cubed pancetta dolce or affumicata (unsmoked or smoked)

1 tbsp Basso extra-virgin olive oil

250g frozen peas

1 x 330g jar of Salsa di Pomodoro Ciliegino (cherry tomato sauce)

500g packet La Molisana no.23 Pennettine

, to serve

Pan fry the pancetta with the oil for 2 to 3 minutes then toss in the peas.

When the peas are cooked, stir in the jar of sauce and simmer until hot.

Meanwhile, cook the pasta according to the packet instructions. When ready, drain well.

Add the pasta to the pan with the pancetta, peas and sauce. Mix well, and serve with shavings of parmesan.

CHICKEN AND VEGETABLE PAPPARDELLE WITH TRUFFLE AND ARTICHOKE PESTO

4 chicken breasts, cut into cubes

1 tbsp Basso extra-virgin olive oil

250g mushrooms, sliced

500g La Molisana no.205 Pappardelle All'uovo

250g green beans, sliced in half

1 x 165g jar of truffle and artichoke pesto

Parmesan, to serve

Pan fry the chicken in the olive oil until cooked (about 5 minutes).

Remove the chicken from the pan and put to one side. Add the mushrooms to the pan with and cook for a few minutes until golden.

Meanwhile, cook the pasta according to the packet instructions. When you have about 5 minutes to go, add the green beans to the pan. When ready, drain both well.

Put the green beans, mushrooms, chicken and pasta in the pan and add the pesto. Mix well, and serve with shavings of parmesan.

Our frozen pizza dough is one of our most popular and best-loved products. The toppings are endless but here are my favourites.

TO PREPARE THE PIZZA DOUGH

Each one of our frozen pizza dough balls makes a ten inch pizza base depending on how thin you like it.

Place the required amount of dough balls on a plate and defrost for around 2-3 hours until soft enough to roll.

Heat the oven to 220°c.

Scatter flour onto a flat work top and roll out your dough to the desired thickness

Place the base on a well-floured baking tray and add your desired pizza toppings.

PIZZA BIANCA RUSTICA

150g fresh Italian fennel sausage

75g fiarelli broccoli

100g smoked Scarmoza cheese, thinly sliced

Extra-virgin olive oil

Chilli flakes (optional)

Skin the fennel sausage, crumble the meat into a pan and fry for about 5 minutes until lightly cooked then scatter onto the pizza base. Add the fiarelli broccoli then the smoked Scarmoza cheese. Ensure all the ingredients are spread evenly and generously over the base.

Place in the heated oven and cook for 5 to10 minutes, checking regularly for desired crispiness.

Drizzle with small amount of olive oil and add chilli flakes if desired, before serving.

THE VEGGIE SPECIAL

4-5 tbsp Mutti Pizza sauce

80g marinated Sicilian artichokes, sliced

80g mixed olives

80g roasted peppers, thinly sliced

100g Gorgonzola cheese, crumbled

4 tsp basil pesto

Spread the pizza sauce onto the prepared pizza base. Scatter over all the vegetables, followed by the gorgonzola and the pesto. Ensure all the ingredients are spread evenly and generously over the base. Place in the heated oven and cook for 5 to10 minutes, checking regularly for desired crispiness.

THE CALABRESE

4-5 tbsp Mutti Pizza sauce

50-80g Calabrian ndjua sausage, skinned

100g roasted peppers, thinly sliced

75g buffalo mozzarella, sliced

Spread the pizza sauce on the prepared pizza bases. Crumble the ndjua sausage and sprinkle over, followed by the roasted peppers then the buffalo mozzarella. Ensure all the ingredients are spread evenly and generously over the base. Place in the heated oven and cook for 5 to10 minutes, checking regularly for desired crispiness.

THE SPICY SPECIAL

4-5 tbsp Mutti pizza sauce

8 slices Ventracina salami

80g strong gorgonzola cheese, crumbled

100g roasted peppers, thinly sliced

Spread the pizza sauce onto the prepared pizza base. Place the Ventracina salami on top followed by the gorgonzola and roasted peppers. Ensure all the ingredients are spread evenly and generously over the base.

Place in the heated oven and cook for 5 to10 minutes, checking regularly for desired crispiness.

Using these delicious ingredients you can make up one of the best antipasto sharing plates for your guests. Just add Italian passion when displaying!

ANTIPASTO SELECTION

2 Buffalo burrata

6-8 large slices Parma ham

3-4 large tomatoes, sliced

6-8 slices Finnochione salami

6-8 slices Ventracina salami

6-8 slices Stoffolotto salami

150g Sicilan marinated artichokes, sliced

150g Pistou olives

150g roasted peppers, sliced

Multigrain and olive bread, sliced, to serve

Home-produced Sicilian olive oil, to serve

I love preparing this for my guests. I always have separate dishes for the Parma ham, fresh tomato and the burrata. Take the burrata out of the fridge at least 30 minutes before eating, and make this the last thing you place on your platter as it tends to break and ooze if left too long. I never slice burrata as it tends to get really messy due to its intense creaminess. Give it all a good drizzle of olive oil before serving.

Then I just put all the salami and marinated vegetables on another dish which also makes it easier to pass the food around.

TRADITIONAL ITALIAN CHEESE BOARD

200g Provolone piccante Auricchio (a lovely, strong pasteurised cow's milk cheese)

200g Pecorino Del Colle (a tasty, semi-mature pasteurised Sardinian sheep's milk cheese)

200g Mountain Gorgonzola (a classic full-flavoured Italian blue)

200g Crucolo (a medium, unpasteurised Piemontese cow's milk cheese with a nice bite)

200g Taleggio (an almost brie-like pasteurised cow's milk cheese with a lovely tang)

OR

200g Camembert di Bufallo (a mild, but full of flavour, creamy buffalo milk cheese. It's availability can be limited due to seasons)

Serve with sweet quince and fig condiment for cheese, and a selection of rosemary and chilli crackers.

INTERNATIONAL CHEESE BOARD

200g Snowdonian Black Bomber cheddar (a lovely pasteurised strong mature Welsh cheese with a creamy tang)

200g Brebrirousse (a soft, creamy, unpasteurised, mild, but full-flavoured French sheep's milk cheese)

200g Montagnola (award-winning German soft, mild, creamy blue cheese)

200g Comte (a classic French unpasteurised strong cow's milk cheese with lots of flavour)

200g Crucolo (a medium unpasteurised Piemontese cows milk cheese with a nice bite)

Serve with damson and quince fruit condiment for cheese and a selection of rosemary and chilli crackers.

COFFEE WITH A SMILE

DELICIOUS COFFEE AND WARM COMPANY HAVE MADE CHARLIE'S COFFEE SHOP AND COFFEE VAN A LOCAL FAVOURITE.

Charlie's Coffee & Company started life over a decade ago serving customers at St Albans station from a coffee van with three wheels; a stop at Charlie's van is a morning ritual for many. Commuters wait in line for their "usuals" served with a sprinkling of morning cheer, then head off with an audible sigh of caffeinated relief.

Charlie's coffee shop on nearby London Road is a light-filled space on the sunny side of the street. The café has a cool and vibrant feel, with plants aplenty and interiors that delight. It's well-rooted in the community and you'll be welcomed with warmth by the friendly crew who've learnt the Charlie's way.

Every inch of this characterful coffee shop is beautifully tiny with wooden tables and concrete lighting that emit a cosy glow. The cheeky twists on wording and fun little quirks add to its much-loved jolly spirit.

Charlie's ethos is considerate with utmost care taken over the company's environmental impact. The shop is powered by renewable energy, the cups are sustainable and they recycle spent coffee grounds into bio-fuel. You won't find mainstream papers in the café and there's no WIFI to encourage connections with people rather than screens.

The café is a hive of activity with dog walkers, nomadic workers, pre-cinema goers and bundled up babies all popping in. It's a place to while away an afternoon people-watching or to slurp tea on the sun-drenched terrace. Coffee aficionados navigate to Charlie's for the prowess of its baristas'; speciality coffee brewed with skill and passion. Charlie's house blend is brewed to precision and silky smooth Guernsey milk is poured by knowledgeable baristas. Coffee paraphernalia adorns the shelves and they stock an impressive selection of speciality beans to take home.

For many, the weekend starts at Charlie's: cyclists meet for a post-Chilterns brew, runners leave their muddy shoes at the door and kids wear Little Charlie's Crew t-shirts ready for hi-fives. Baristas toe-tap to the music and dance through the coffee-machine steam, as punters queue for the stone-baked pastries, sourdough toast with jam or toasted banana bread with lashings of butter. The counter is filled to the brim with cakes baked by small-scale producers passionate about provenance, and their house-made sarnies are a popular choice.

Charlie's has evolved over the years to stand the test of time but it is the constants that make Charlie's what it is: a business run with care and authenticity, morals as strong as the coffee and a sense of humour at heart. You leave here better than when you arrived.

A TASTY CUP OF COFFEE

This recipe is to help take your morning brew to a tastier level using the humble cafètiere. There are many variables in making a great cup of coffee at home so have a go at changing elements around to get your perfect cup.

YOU WILL NEED

Cafètiere/French press

Scales

Fresh coffee beans

Burr grinder

Kettle

Timer

A NOTE ON WATER

Your brewed coffee consists mainly of water so try to use filtered or treated water for best results. Use water just off the boil (waiting 30 seconds will do the trick).

A NOTE ON GRINDERS

Grinding your coffee just before brewing will prevent the aroma from fading. For best results use a burr (not blade) grinder (an adjustable manual or electric grinder). Grinders vary widely depending on the manufacturer but a simple burr grinder will be a step up from buying pre-ground coffee.

WHAT IS A CAFÈTIERE?

Otherwise known as a French press or plunger, a cafètiere is one of the most popular and classic brewing methods due to its simplicity and classic design. Coffee grounds are separated from water by a mesh filter producing a bold, full-bodied and full-flavoured cup.

BEANS

Start with fresh beans roasted within the past 2 weeks or so if possible. If you want a really tasty cup of coffee then buy your beans from a place that cares about the beans they sell. Look out for a variety of origins on the shelves, baristas who can recommend beans for your tastes and always look out for roast dates. Try to buy beans as close to the roast date as possible for maximum yum.

Try using coffee from different countries, origins and farms until you find the flavour notes you like in your cup. You may prefer a fruity cup of coffee with heaps of zesty brightness or you may prefer chocolatey, nutty or sweeter caramel notes; this is a personal preference and taste is very subjective, so go with what tastes good for you.

Once home, treat your coffee like any other fresh product and don't keep it too long. Store your coffee in an airtight container, or in a sealed bag with a clip in a cool, dry place.

BREWING

Put the cafètiere on the scales and tare the scales to zero. Fill the cafètiere with cold tap water and weigh the capacity of your cafètiere (1 gram = 1ml). Multiply the capacity of your cafètiere by 0.07 to get the amount of coffee you'll need (70g of coffee per litre of water).

Weigh your beans out on the scales and grind as above or ask your local coffee shop to grind it to a 'coarse cafètiere grind' for you.

Boil your kettle (using filtered water if possible). Preheat your cafètiere and mugs by pouring in a small volume of water from the just boiled kettle.

Put the coffee in the cafètiere. Pour just enough water to cover the grounds and leave for 30 seconds to 'bloom'. When water hits the ground coffee it releases gases present in the coffee. The fresher the beans the more gas will be released and the bigger the frothy crust will be on top of the coffee. A frothy bloom is a good sign and a flat or lifeless bloom can indicate that the beans are old.

Add the rest of the water and set a timer for 4 minutes. Plunge slowly and then pour into your preheated mugs. Add milk if you'd like but try it black first.

Preparation time: 5 minutes | Brewing time: 4 minutes

FLAVOUR WITH FLAIR

A LIGHT, MODERN APPROACH TO CLASSIC INDIAN RECIPES HAS MADE CHILLI BAR A FAVOURITE IN ST ALBANS.

Kashim's family have owned restaurants in Hertfordshire for years; he learned the business first-hand at his father's restaurants in Bushey and Hoddesdon before going on to work with his brother at Chilli Raj in Fleetville. Kashim opened Chilli Bar and Kitchen just along from the Clock Tower in central St Albans in 2012, and it has been busy ever since.

Before it was Chilli Bar and Kitchen, the building was home to Barney's bar, and Kashim decided to keep an area of the restaurant for drinks so people could head there before sitting down for dinner. The interior is light and spacious with pale cream walls with a subtle paisley print picked out in gold to add a warm feel, and funky bright lights to add splashes of colour, and was designed by one of Kashim's customers.

Kashim explained that the menu includes favourites from the Indian subcontinent, with many dishes from Bangladesh, Kashmir and Bengal. You will find fish, lamb, and chicken dishes on the menu, along with lots of delicious vegetarian dishes, and you can certainly eat very well if you want vegan and veggie:

Navatoan jalfrezi, Kombi piazza as well as the vegetable tray (a little like a thali) are popular. Laal maans, a rich lamb curry, was only introduced to the menu last year and has become the most popular dish on the menu (you can see it over the page). The team of chefs work hard to prep everything from scratch (they get through about 400kg of onions each week!) and if you have dietary requirements they can adapt a recipe for you and tell you what is in everything. Kashim uses local suppliers where possible, including vegetables from nearby Jersey Farm.

In 2018 Chilli Bar and Kitchen appeared on Channel S (Sky 734), in a competition to create a delicious, healthy dish. They won the challenge with their salmon, asparagus and basmati rice dish, which used steam to keep the dish light and full of flavour. More locally, they have also been named best local restaurant three years running by the St Albans Curry Club!

LAAL MAANS

Laal maans is a very popular curry, traditionally from Rajasthan, India. It is usually made with mutton or lamb. The sauce is rich with yoghurt and hot spices.

FOR THE PASTE

8 dry red chillies

2 tbsp fresh coriander seeds

½ tsp turmeric powder

1 tbsp garlic paste

FOR THE MARINADE

245g natural yoghurt

500g lamb chops

FOR THE ONIONS

4 tbsp vegetable oil

4 medium onions, thinly sliced

TO FINISH

Salt, to taste

1 tsp garam masala powder

4 tbsp finely chopped coriander leaves

FOR THE PASTE

Place the chillies and coriander seeds in a bowl of water and allow them to soak for 10 minutes. Drain them and place in a food processor. Add the turmeric powder and garlic paste. Whizz together, adding a couple tablespoons of water at a time to form a paste.

FOR THE MARINADE

Mix the paste with the natural yoghurt to make a marinade and then spoon over the chops, coating well. Leave the meat to marinate in it for 1 hour.

FOR THE ONIONS

Meanwhile, heat the vegetable oil in a large pan and add the onions. Cook over a medium heat, stirring to avoid burning. Once the onions turn golden brown, use a slotted spoon to remove the onions and place them on a plate covered in kitchen roll. Lightly dab the kitchen roll over the onions to remove excess oil. Put the onions into a food processor and whizz to make a smooth paste.

TO FINISH

Reusing the oil left over from frying the onions, add the onion paste to it and fry it for 2 minutes. Then add the meat and its marinade and allow it to fry until the oil begins to separate from the sauce. Stir frequently and whenever the sauce starts to stick to the pan, sprinkle over a little bit of water. Then season with salt.

Once the meat is properly cooked, remove the pan from the heat and sprinkle garam masala over it. Garnish with fresh coriander before serving with chapatis, naan or rice.

Preparation time: 1 hour 15 minutes | Cooking time: 25 minutes | Serves: 2

LIQUID GOLD

RIGHT ON THE EDGE OF THE CHILTERNS, YET STILL IN HERTFORDSHIRE, YOU WILL BE ABLE TO SPOT THE BRIGHT YELLOW FIELDS OF RAPESEED IN THE SUMMER THAT PRODUCE CHILTERN COLD PRESSED OIL

Simon and Chris are fifth generation farmers from the Mead family who have been farming in the Chilterns since 1860. "We are a traditional mixed farm with arable, cattle and sheep. We believe that mixed farms help support sustainable farming practises which are beneficial to both the farmer and the surrounding environment, encouraging local wildlife to thrive."

The distinctive golden yellow oil is comparable to the best extra-virgin olive oil; as well as having a delicious flavour, it is rich in omega 3, 6 and 9 and vitamin E. It contains no artificial flavourings or preservatives and is ideal for cooking as well as making dressings and marinades. It has a higher smoking point than olive oil so is more suitable for heating at high temperatures, making it ideal for roasting and shallow frying. You might also like to know that it is low in cholesterol, and is lower in saturated fats than olive oil and butter.

The rapeseed is harvested in late July, dried, cleaned and stored in the grain store to keep it in perfect condition until pressing. The cold pressing method is a traditional technique which gently squeezes the oil from the seeds. This gentle process ensures the full flavour and nutritional content of the oil is preserved. It is then filtered and bottled on the farm. The waste seed after pressing is fed to the Aberdeen Angus herd who live on the farm.

Sold all over Hertfordshire and beyond, you will find Chiltern Cold Pressed in the farm's own shop, and also at Wayside Farm in King's Langley, Sunnyside Rural Trust in Hemel and Carpenters in St Albans. They also show at the Herts County show and at local food festivals including Letchworth and Hitchin. Matt Baker and the Countryfile team visited the farm in 2016 to make a feature about the farm and its award-winning oils (they have won many Great Taste Gold awards).

Look out for the infusion range of oils which includes chilli, garlic, oak-smoked, rosemary, lemon, orange and porcini, which you can use to make salad dressings, marinades or amazing roast potatoes and vegetables. Lemon and smoked mayonnaise (as well as classic) retain the amazing golden yellow colours, and are packed with nutrients as well as flavour. As the farm shop business has grown over the years, the family have also created salad dressings and BBQ sauces.

GOLDEN ROAST POTATOES

Chiltern cold-pressed rapeseed oil produces the most wonderful roast potatoes when using the plain oil. If you would like to flavour them up use the rosemary, thyme and garlic oil, or if you want a little kick, use the chilli oil.
You can use any great roasting potato; Maris Piper, King Edward or any red-skinned variety will work well.

1kg potatoes, peeled and cut into the size you like

100ml Chiltern cold-pressed oil of your choice

Freshly ground black pepper and sea salt

Preheat the oven to 180°c.

Put the potatoes into a pan of boiling water and cook for about 5 minutes until the outsides start to become soft.

Meanwhile, pour the oil into a roasting tray and place in the preheated oven.

Drain the water from the pan, leaving the potatoes in the saucepan. Gently shake the saucepan to roughen up the edges of the potatoes.

Put the potatoes in the hot roasting tin and shake to coat well in the hot oil. Season to taste with plenty of black pepper and sea salt. Space out the potatoes and place them back in the oven.

After about 1 hour the potatoes will be golden and ready to eat. Garnish with fresh or dried herbs if you wish.

Preparation time: *10 minutes* | Cooking time: *40 minutes* | Serves *4*

COBBLED TOGETHER

AT THE COBBLED KITCHEN, PEOPLE LEARN TO BE INSTINCTIVE COOKS AND GET BACK TO FEELING EMPOWERED AND ENTHUSIASTIC ABOUT COOKING.

When Danielle was a child, if she asked her mum what was for dinner that night, she'd reply, "Oh, some concoction.' And that was normal. Something delicious would be cobbled together out of nowhere and nothing."

We now have lots of television programmes and recipe books to tell us how to cook, and many of us have lost confidence in following our own cooking instincts. As Danielle says, "here in the West, although baking has enjoyed a massive revival, there has been a decline in cooking main meals from scratch since the supermarkets started convincing us we don't have time to cook and that they would take over that arduous task for us."

In her home-based cookery school, between Harpenden and St Albans, Danielle creates a relaxed atmosphere where people of all ages can talk about food, share ideas and grow in confidence about 'cobbling' together something delicious to eat. Danielle set up The Cobbled Kitchen in 2014 with the belief that if people could see someone throwing ingredients together without measuring or timing, adding a little creative flair, and the confident knowledge that it will turn out delicious and beautiful, those same instinctive skills would rub off.

Clients leave the classes feeling empowered and enthusiastic about cooking. They all muck in, practice their slicing and chopping, have the chance to choose what goes in next, taste, stir, rescue what was forgotten in the oven, share their concerns and foodie fears, and ultimately have a good laugh. You also get to take home what you've cooked!

Danielle has some lovely advice for anyone about to try some of the recipes in this book:

"Although I'm nestled in this book amongst many fantastic chefs and food producers in our wonderful Hertfordshire, I'd like you to try looking at all these recipes as mere starting points for making your food. If it doesn't turn out exactly like these amazing photos, if you've followed the recipe to the letter but it hasn't turned out quite how you expected, then, you're not a failed cook! You simply need to read between the lines of the recipe. It does matter that you make something look and taste good, so think about how to do so in your own way. Ask yourself; should I slice these courgettes into discs like always, or try more interesting pointy chunks so they catch a little more colour and therefore flavour? If I cooked this sauce for longer, would it be thicker and shinier than if I follow the timings stated in the recipe…? I am sure it will be equally delicious!"

THE COBBLED KITCHEN

the art of instinctive cooking

Danielle designs the classes around the client's wishes, and she often goes to people's homes so they can work with their own stuff. One day it might be stressed parents who are cooking two or three different dinners for their family's multiple tastes and needs. Other days she works with men who want to cook more to contribute to family life or are feeding themselves for the first time since becoming widowed. There are also many young adults who leave home unable to feed themselves, so, they tell Danielle what they like to eat, what they'd like to be able to make, and that's what they do, together. Here are some of Danielle's top tips for becoming a more relaxed and instinctive cook:

KNIFE SKILLS

Nearly every dish starts with a chopped onion or requires something to be sliced or diced. Learning how to chop easily and safely saves you time later, and you soon realise that how you use the knife makes such a difference! You don't need the latest, most expensive kit – Danielle's kitchen knives are a hotch-potch collection from over the years that do everything – they serve as crushers, scoopers, scrapers and pokers!

MOTHER NATURE GIVES THE CLUES

Look at an onion closely. How has it grown? How can I use its structure to my advantage? See how there are fine lines, almost ridges underneath the discarded peel? All this is Mother Nature telling you to slice lengthways for when you want a sliced onion – going across, well that's just going against the grain! A clove of garlic will reveal its wonderful pale flesh willingly if you respect its physiology. Just cut off the root end, lay the knife flat over the garlic, press down firmly, pinch the tip, poke the exposed flesh and pull apart!

WASTE LESS AND MAKE FRESH FOODS LAST LONGER

We should all fall in love again with leftovers, and think of ways to use everything we buy. (Potato peelings make healthy crisps!) Even if you work all hours, whether on your own or part of a family, you can eat fresh and healthy every day. Plant-based vitamins and fibre (herbs, salads and vegetables) live longer if you treat them like the plants they are – like a bunch of cut flowers – cut the stem/base, sit in water, cover and leave in the fridge. They will last so much longer!

A GOOD STORE CUPBOARD IS YOUR PAINTER'S PALETTE

Pastes, pestos, jellies, tapenades, vinegars, reduced fruit syrups, dried herbs and spices are all useful additions to any dish. They help develop flavour, texture or colour and even if a recipe doesn't mention them, use them to help achieve the desired end results. Don't worry about their use-by dates as they're all steeped in sugar, salt or vinegar, which renders them (almost) immortal! The broader the contents of your larder and fridge, the more scope you have to create anything at all.

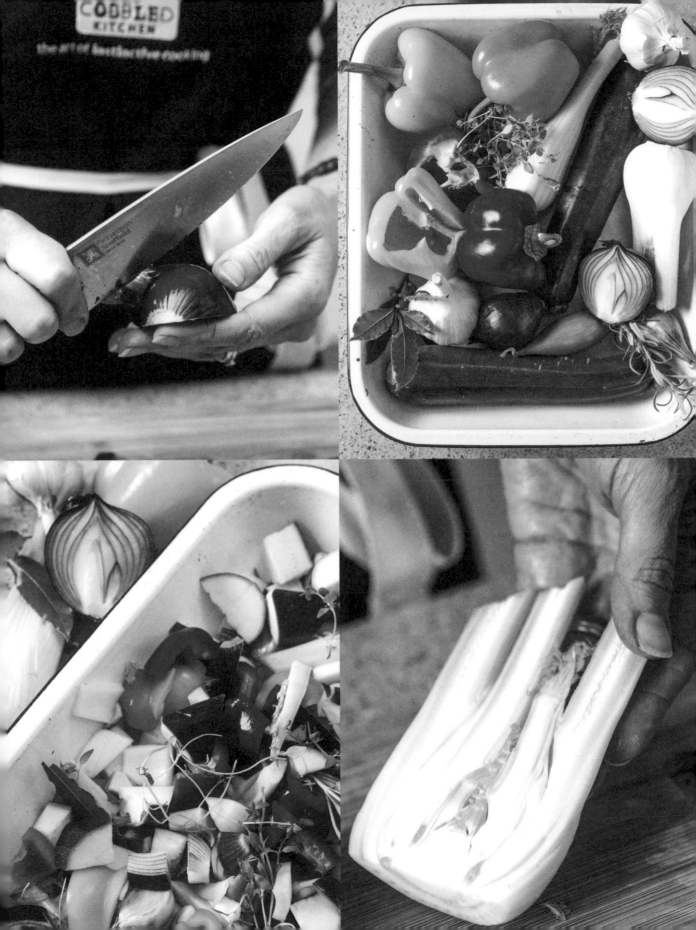

'FLEXITARIAN' TRAY BAKE

For when you need to feed the vegan, carnivore and vegetarian in your life, all at once and quickly! The ingredients used here are just what I happened to have in my fridge and larder. Tap into your instinctive creativity to use whatever will give a balance of flavour and colour.

FOR THE ROASTED VEGETABLE BASE

1 red onion

2 or 3 peppers, any colour

1 courgette

1 small fennel bulb

6 cloves of garlic

3 sprigs of woody herbs such as rosemary and thyme

1-2 bay leaves

2 tbsp good olive oil

Freshly ground black pepper and sea salt

Balsamic vinegar glaze, to drizzle

FOR THE PROTEIN TOPPING, YOUR CHOICE OF:

1 chicken breast

2 fish fillets, with skin on

250g (one packet) halloumi

225g (one packet) plain or smoked tofu

1 tbsp pesto, tapenade or bruschetta, for spreading

Chilli flakes (optional)

1 tbsp breadcrumbs, fresh or frozen

1-2 vines of cherry tomatoes

Olive oil, to drizzle

Preheat the oven to 200°c Roughly chop the vegetables into similar sized chunks making sure they have some pointy corners (these will catch some colour and crispness better than flat discs).

Throw the vegetables into a large roasting tray and add the garlic cloves (with their skins on) and the herbs. Add the olive oil and season well with salt and pepper. Mix together and shake the tray so everything settles evenly. Drizzle a little balsamic glaze over the vegetables and place the tray in the oven for 15 minutes or until there are some golden charred edges to the vegetables.

Meanwhile, cut the halloumi and/or tofu into slices, a similar thickness to the fish fillets. Cut the chicken into two or three escalopes, if using. Choose your topping to spread over the halloumi, tofu, chicken or fish. Use the same topping for everything or mix and match; it's up to you!' Sprinkle some breadcrumbs over the topping on the chicken or fish and drizzle with a little oil to help prevent them from burning. A pinch of chilli flakes on the halloumi is pretty and delicious!

Remove the tray from the oven and carefully lay the chicken, fish, halloumi and/or tofu on top of the roasted vegetables. Place a vine of cherry tomatoes or two in between and place the whole tray back in the oven for another 10 to 12 minutes or until the chicken is cooked thoroughly but the fish isn't over cooked.

Place the tray bake in the centre of the table for all to help themselves to their favourites. Serve with a green salad and crusty bread with which you can soak up the juices at the bottom of the roasting pan.

Take this recipe 'with a pinch of salt': do your own thing, use whatever you need to use up, change the flavours from Mediterranean to Middle Eastern if you want. Just make it tasty and beautiful.

Preparation time: 10 minutes | Cooking time: 20-25 minutes | Serves 4-6

THE LOCALS' SECRET

TUCKED AWAY IN A PRETTY COURTYARD, THIS FAMILY-RUN CAFÉ SERVES DELICIOUS HOMEMADE BREAKFASTS, LUNCHES AND CAKES, WHERE REGULARS RETURN TIME AND AGAIN.

Walk past the herb garden and step through the beautiful arched doorway into The Courtyard Café, and you will be delighted you discovered it. A beautiful light space, filled with art, funky homewares and excellent homemade food, the café draws many regulars away from the coffee chains in St Albans city centre.

Julie and Michael opened the café on Hatfield Road about 10 years ago and they now have many regulars, including people from the yoga hall next door, Radio Verulam presenters from upstairs, artists, writers' groups and a ukulele group to name just a few! There is always a warm welcome from the team, who have known some of their regulars from childhood.

Walls are lined with prints and paintings by local artists, including Julie, who also painted the stunning mural behind the sofa. Windowsills and shelves are filled with vintage and quirky homeware, including plants, candles, plates and Scandinavian cloths and bags.

You will spot the cake counter when you walk in, and it is hard to resist. The cakes are made by the team in-house and change all the time; you might see lime and coconut drizzle, rose and pistachio, barm brack, vegan mocha cake or sticky toffee banoffee (there is always at least one gluten-free cake).

The breakfast and lunch menus are written on chalkboards around the counter, with seasonal specials too. Breakfast and brunch runs all day, and could be a full veggie, a Mexican omelette, a thick slice of granary toast with avocado or free-range eggs, or yoghurt with granola and honey.

Lunch has an international feel and the team have chosen dishes that are packed with flavour. There is always a homemade soup, which you can have with mackerel paté too. Mixed bean and halloumi salad or dahl with chutney are favourites, as are the hearty open sandwiches such as the Scandi, with beetroot humous, smoked salmon and dill pickle.

Michael and Julie have always supported local suppliers, as well as artists, and the granola is from Dizzy Bee, the granary bread is from Redbournbury Mill and the ice cream from Darlish.

On a sunny day, grab a table outside and enjoy the suntrap courtyard, and if you need to book a space for a private vintage tea, or get on with some work, then the lovely back room is a cosy spot, whatever the weather. A lovely, local indie that always makes delicious food.

MIDDLE EASTERN CAKE

This delicious cake is hugely popular in The Courtyard Café. It has a wonderful consistency, just the right amount of sweetness and spice, and a sticky, nutty top. It's really great with a good morning coffee or a cuppa in the afternoon.

FOR THE CAKE

250g butter, chopped

1 tbsp grated orange zest

55g caster sugar

4 medium eggs

150g self-raising flour

¼ tsp baking powder

2 tsp ground cinnamon

125g ground almonds

135g desiccated coconut

60g chopped pecans

180ml orange juice

20g flaked almonds

Pecan halves, to decorate

FOR THE SYRUP

220g caster sugar

160ml orange juice

Preheat the oven to 180°c. Grease a deep 23cm loose-bottomed cake tin and line it with baking parchment.

Beat the butter, orange zest and sugar in a large bowl with an electric mixer until light and fluffy. Add the eggs one at a time, beating well between additions.

Sift the flour and stir it into the mixture with the baking powder, cinnamon, ground almonds, coconut and chopped pecans. Stir in the orange juice.

Spread the mixture into the prepared tin, sprinkle with the flaked almonds and arrange the pecans halves around the edge of the cake and in the centre.

Bake in the preheated oven for about 45 minutes.

Meanwhile, make the syrup. Combine the sugar and juice in a pan and stir over a low heat without boiling until the sugar has dissolved. Then turn up the heat and boil the syrup, without stirring, for about 5 minutes until thickened. When the cake is baked, pour the hot syrup over the hot cake while in the tin, and then leave the cake to cool completely, before releasing from the tin. The cake is delicious with a dollop of real Greek yoghurt.

Preparation time: 15 minutes, plus cooling time | Cooking time: 45 minutes | Makes 10 slices

DELICIOUSLY HEALTHY

BAKED IN SMALL BATCHES, USING ONLY THE VERY BEST NATURAL INGREDIENTS, DIZZY BEE GRANOLA IS A BREAKFAST FAVOURITE ALL OVER HERTFORDSHIRE!

Nicky Halloran started Dizzy Bee Granola because she couldn't find a granola that she was happy to give to her young family. So she experimented with making her own, and this lead to a delicious range of granolas that she sold at farmers' markets and is now found in kitchens all across Hertfordshire and the UK.

You can spot the distinctive bright yellow bags with the bee motif in lots of local shops and cafés around Hertfordshire; choose from Nourishingly Nutty, Gluten-free Pecan and Quinoa or Coconutty, which is a low-carb granola and is the latest to hit the shelves. Word has spread and Dizzy Bee has won a Great Taste Award every year since 2014 and a total of nine Gold Great Taste Stars stars overall.

Nicky wanted to make a deliciously balanced breakfast free from anything artificial, that would provide a healthy boost of nutrients, rather than a huge sugar rush. The granolas start with wholegrain oats from Cambridgeshire sweetened with a little honey or maple (depending on flavour) and are baked with sumptuous Chiltern cold-pressed rapeseed oil that is grown and produced at Mead Farm near Berkhamstead. Mixtures of sunflower, pumpkin, sesame, flax, and chia seeds are added, some finely ground, so you get a rich source of protein and seedy goodness in each mouthful. The protein means that the granola is filling too, so you should have the energy you need to get you through a busy morning. Generous amounts of nuts and berries are added to each batch and Nicky spent months getting the balance of each recipe just right. Nicky formerly worked as a chef including location catering for TV and running her own café.

You can eat the moreish granola by the bowlful, with whatever milk or fruit juice you like, or sprinkle it over yoghurt or porridge; whatever you like to make your breakfast more delicious. Dizzy Bee often appears on breakfast menus in cafés such as The Courtyard Café, The Fleetville Larder, George Street Canteen, Pudding Stop, Smokehouse Deli, Hatch, Street Café and Fade to Black.

Nicky has also developed Busy Bars, which pop up for sale in healthfood shops, cafés and train stations around Herts. Both the Fruit & Nut and the Cacao Busy Bars are vegan and 100% natural, and are made with mainly seeds and nuts and are grain-free to give you that slow release of energy.

Made with that personal touch and the best high quality ingredients available, Dizzy Bee is the perfect way to start your mornings. If you want to try it for yourself, pick up a bag at Carpenters Farm Shop in Sandridge, B Healthy in St Albans, Charlie's coffee (and many of the cafés already mentioned!), Farm Butchery In Codicote or buy it from The Refill Pantry in St Albans where you can take your own container along. You will definitely be back for more!

APRICOT AND ALMOND GRANOLA

A deliciously indulgent granola, perfect to make for weekend brunch with friends. The chia, sunflower, flax, pumpkin and almonds provide super-nutritional gains to boot. Serve with bowls of yoghurt and fruit or just with your favourite milk. Granola is one of the most flexible and easy things you can cook, so if you don't like an ingredient, just swap it for something you do!

110ml rapeseed oil, coconut oil or olive oil (we use Chiltern cold-pressed rapeseed oil from Tring)

140g sweetener of your choice (honey, maple or date syrup)

330g oats

50g sunflower seeds

30g pumpkin seeds

20g ground flaxseed

20g white chia seeds

50g flaked or whole almonds (whichever you prefer)

½ tsp ground cinnamon

Pinch of ground nutmeg

100g organic soft apricots, chopped into small pieces (or any dried fruit you like)

Preheat the oven to 140°c fan.

Place the oil and sweetener in a saucepan and gently heat until melted; do not boil.

Meanwhile, place all the dry ingredients apart from apricots in a large bowl and mix well.

Pour the oil and sweetener mixture into the dry mixture and stir until all coated thoroughly.

Line a large baking sheet with greaseproof paper and put the mixture in the tray, about 1cm thick. Flatten with the back of a spatula. If you need to, use two baking trays rather than overfill.

Place in the oven, and bake for 20 minutes. Take out the tray, turn over the granola gently with a spatula, spread the mix out gently and place back in for another 15 to 20 minutes until golden and crunchy; check after 15 minutes, as the granola can easily overcook in the last 5 minutes.

Take out and leave to cool; do not stir again until it is cool, as this will help crunchy clusters form.

When the granola is cool add the apricots or your choice of dried fruit.

Store in an airtight container or Kilner jar and your granola will keep for up to a month this way.

A NOTE ON SALT

We really feel there is enough salt in food already so have not added it here. However, if you like a bit of salty sweet, just add a few sprinkles of seasalt to your dry mix before baking.

Preparation time: 10 minutes | Cooking time: 45 minutes | Makes 6 servings or sprinkle over yoghurt

FARR OUT

FROM BREWING THEIR OWN AWARD-WINNING CRAFT BEERS TO REVITALISING OLD PUBS, THE FARR BREW TEAM HAVE BEEN VERY BUSY!

Nick and Matt started Farr Brew just six years ago and their impact on the local beer and pub scene has been dramatic. Their plan, "to make great tasting beer and bring it to the public" has certainly worked and they now run a brewery, tap room and four pubs, as well as being familiar faces to anyone who goes to local food festivals and events. They have won multiple awards for their beer, environmental efforts, service to the community and as a top producer in Hertfordshire.

The Brewery Tap Room on Coleman Green Lane was their first venue, where they hold tasting events, summer barbecues, beer festivals and brewery tours. The beers are all made here, and alongside bestselling Our Greatest Golden, you can also try Best Bitter, Perfect Pale and Potent Porter plus seasonal specials.

The Reading Rooms 'micropub' in Wheathampstead opened in 2018 in a Grade II-listed building. You can buy Farr Brew on draft to drink in or take home, as well as cider, wine and local gin plus locally produced tea, coffee and cake so there's something for everyone. Sausage rolls and Scotch eggs are made by Brimark Butchers, just down the road.

The Rising Sun in Slip End re-opened in 2019, and they have an excellent food menu now that Farr Brew have more space to play with. Venison sausage with mash, roasted seasonal fowl and mushroom stroganoff means that everyone eats well. The Red Cow in Harpenden joined Farr Brew in 2019 and the latest pub, The Eight Bells, is just a short walk down from Hatfield House, in old Hatfield.

Working with other indies is something the Farr Brew team enjoy, and they have made beer for many people including Rothamsted, using their own grains, and Black Listed IBA for Ye Olde Fighting Cocks. The Reading Rooms has hosted tasting sessions in the upstairs room for Blackbridge gin, made in Wheathampstead. You will also see Farr Brew pop up in many local delis and farm shops, and on the menu in restaurants and bars, often in the recipes! Farr Brew are also regulars at local farmers' markets, county shows and food festivals such as Kimpton, Redbourn, Harpenden and St Albans as well as the Childwickbury Christmas market (their Brewdolph is a Christmas stocking essential).

MATT KEMP, RED COW PUB - HARPENDEN
THE GOLDEN BELLY

This rich, warming dish is perfect for those cold winter evenings with family or friends. For best results, the pork belly should be left to marinate in the rub overnight. We use high-welfare pork from our local farmer, fed on Farr Brew spent brewer's grains.

1.5kg rectangle cut of pork belly

1 cooking apple, peeled and cut into 1cm slices

1 white onion, peeled and cut into 1cm slices

2 ribs of celery, chopped

5 cloves of garlic

1 tsp juniper berries

3 bay leaves

700ml Farr Brew Greatest Golden Ale

1 tbsp sea salt flakes

1.5kg Maris Piper potatoes, peeled and cut into medium-sized chunks

80g salted butter

2 tbsp double cream

2 tbsp wholegrain mustard

2–3 fennel bulbs, cut into 1cm slices widthways

50ml orange juice

Olive oil, for cooking

Freshly ground black pepper

Sage leaves, for decoration

FOR THE RUB

2 tbsp olive oil

1 tbsp ground pepper

1 tbsp sea salt

1 tbsp ground white fennel seeds

Place the pork belly skin side up in a dish and score with a sharp knife. Combine the rub ingredients and massage the rub firmly into the skin. Cover and refrigerate overnight.

Preheat the oven to 175°c.

Put the onion and apple in the base of a deep roasting tray (about 32cm in length). Add the celery, four of the garlic cloves, the juniper berries and bay leaves to the roasting dish.

Place your pork belly skin side up in the tray (make sure you cover the garlic cloves). Pour the Farr Brew Golden Ale into the base of roasting dish so the pork is sitting in the beer but not submerged.

Splash a little olive oil over the skin, scatter with salt flakes and put in the oven (uncovered) on the middle shelf for 2 hours 30 minutes. After this time, turn the heat up to 200°c for a further 30 minutes to finish and crisp up the skin.

Meanwhile, start to prepare everything else. Bring a large saucepan of water to the boil and add the potatoes. Cook for about 15 to 20 minutes until softened. Drain into a colander and return to the pan on a low heat for a few minutes to dry up any excess water.

Add salt and pepper, butter and double cream then mash potatoes thoroughly. Stir in mustard and check seasoning.

Place a large frying pan on a low heat, add a knob of butter and the remaining garlic clove then add the fennel and cook for around 5 to 10 minutes until softened. Add a little olive oil and turn up the heat to crisp the fennel. Add the orange juice and cook until caramelised and fennel is fully coated. Remove the fennel and fry the sage leaves for a minute until crispy.

Remove the pork and leave to rest, keeping the juices for the sauce.

Remove the bay leaves and juniper berries from the pork roasting tray and pour the contents of tray into a blender. Blitz and pour into a large saucepan. Season to taste and cook on a medium heat until reduced to a thicker sauce, stirring frequently. Add any additional juices from the resting meat.

Slice the pork belly and place on top of the mash along with the fennel. Top with the sauce and finish with the fried sage leaves.

ALL STOCKED UP

EVER-CHANGING DELI AND BUSY CAFÉ BY DAY, QUIRKY BAR AT NIGHT, THE FLEETVILLE LARDER PACKS A LOT INTO ITS SMALL SPACE

Although only open since 2017, The Fleetville Larder, just a short walk from St Albans train station and beautiful Clarence Park, already feels like a favourite neighbour. If you need a place to take a break from work, to meet friends, buy some groceries or grab a takeaway coffee, this cosy deli and café has fast become a hub in the community.

The vibe created by Ed is warm and welcoming, with reclaimed wooden benches and school chairs, and customers share the tables to try and squeeze in (there is only space for about 20). Walls are lined with interesting food and drink, often from local suppliers, You will be able to spot local favourites such as Campfire Gin, Farr Brew, Mad Squirrel Beer and Dizzy Bee Granola along with a mix of European and British deli staples including olive oils, pasta, jams, cookies and chocolates. The larder's eclectic wines include interesting grape varities such as Bonarda, Pecorino and Pais which Ed is on hand to talk you through .

Cheese fills the counter, and is the focus of the Larder. British artisan cheeses such as Colston Bassett Stilton, Irish Gubbeen, Montgomery's Cheddar and Kirkhams Lancashire sit alongside European classics such as Mature Comté, Aged Gouda and Manchego. You can buy just a slice or a whole cheese, which many customers do, especially in the run up to Christmas. Interesting crackers from Peter's Yard and Zingiberi Bakery and chutneys to go with your cheese fill whole shelves, so you can find the perfect match for your cheeseboard. Look for Virginia's Kitchen preserves, which are made locally, and are also used in the café's own sandwiches. If you need further inspiration, there is a shelf of cheese books to look through!

You can get a decent cup of tea or coffee (from Tiki Tonga) and cake or sourdough toast at any time of the day. The large print of a grilled cheese sandwich on the wall tells you the deli's speciality, and they have a great choice of toasties, including The Alpine, which is made with raclette cheese, salami, onion and caraway jam. They also serve some interesting salads: one must try is the zingy orange, carrot and watercress with halloumi. Vegans are catered for with olive and garlic bruschetta, or avo-on-toast with lime and coriander.

Evenings take on a different feel and locals pop in to share a bottle of wine and a cheeseboard, often on their way back from the train station. You can also book the Larder for private get-togethers, and they often hold gin, wine and cheese tastings, and have even hosted film showings.

BAKED TUNWORTH

Used here is a Tunworth Cheese, made in Hampshire, which Raymond Blanc has called "the world's best Camembert" but Camembert will work as well.

250g whole Tunworth Cheese in the box
Clove of garlic, peeled and halved
Dash of white wine
Sprig of rosemary

TO SERVE
Gherkins
Charcuterie
Boiled baby potatoes
Fresh crusty bread

Preheat the oven to 200°c.

Take the cheese from the box and remove the paper. Return the cheese to the box.

Prick the cheese several times with a fork. Drizzle over a few drops of the white wine, and rub the surface with the clove of garlic.

Stud the cheese with a few small sprigs of rosemary.

Replace the lid of the box and bake in the oven for 25-30 minutes, until the cheese is bubbling.

Serve direct from the oven, and serve with gherkins and charcuterie, and dip in the potatoes, or scoop up with crusty bread.

Preparation time: 5 minutes | Cooking time: 25 minutes | Serves 2 to share

THE BEE'S KNEES

TUCKED AWAY ON PRETTY GEORGE STREET IN THE HEART OF ST ALBANS' CATHEDRAL QUARTER, THIS FAMILY-RUN CAFÉ IS A LOCALS' SECRET, FOR THEIR DELICIOUS BRUNCHES AND GORGEOUS CATHEDRAL VIEWS.

Julie and Kevin haven't stopped since they started Canteen in 2015. Right from the start they wanted to be at the heart of the community, and they welcome everyone to their quirky café, just a few moments walk from the Clock Tower. Look for the white arch halfway down George Street and head through past the stained glass door to grab one of the retro formica tables inside, or find a cosy spot in the sheltered courtyard.

Brunch is served all day, and there is something for everyone, whether you just want a decent cup of coffee, a yoghurt with granola and berries, or a full English or Mediterranean Breakfast (see over the page!).

Local is everything here. Vegetables and fruits are from Sparshotts, bread is from Dolce Forno, goat's cheese is from Wobbly Bottom Farm in Hitchin and the halloumi is from Lewis of London, nearby in Barnet. Dizzy Bee granola tops the yoghurt pots, and many of the cakes are from Heaven is a Cupcake. Coffee is from Tiki Tonga, another Hertfordshire company.

Soups and sandwiches keep the nearby office workers happy at lunch (there is always a fresh soup of the day) and check out the specials board for something seasonal, whether a Greek salad in the summer, a butternut squash risotto in the autumn or a cranberry and turkey melt in the run up to Christmas.

If you are quick you can pick up a jar of their own honey, collected from hives tucked away at the back of the café. Delicious, amber-gold, and not too sweet, this honey can be eaten by the spoonful, but the café also uses it in its baking and for special events such as the recent Beebeque, where locally sourced meats were marinated in the honey before grilling and the cocktails were honey-based.

George Street has a buzzy, community feel where the indie businesses support each other. Chefs from nearby restaurants are regulars for Canteen's cooked breakfasts, before heading off to work. At the Gin and Jazz festival in Autumn, Canteen served cocktails and barbecued sausages and halloumi to DJ dance beats while people packed out the courtyard strung with white lights.

In the summer, head to the walled garden, past the mural painted on the café walls of the beehives, bees and flowers to discover the most amazing Cathedral views.

Homemade biscuits and water bowls are ready to welcome dogs after a walk around Verulamium park; no-one leaves Canteen hungry.

MEDITERRANEAN BREAKFAST

We chose this dish because it's one of the most popular dishes we make at the café. It's a great alternative cooked breakfast to our full English. It can also easily be made vegetarian by swapping the chorizo for halloumi.

2 sweet potatoes, cut into wedges

Drizzle of rapeseed oil

Freshly ground black pepper and salt, to taste

2 good quality chorizo sausages (each about 70g)

1 bunch of cherry tomatoes on the vine

Splash of white wine vinegar

4 medium eggs

1 avocado

½ lemon

Tabasco sauce, to taste

Preheat the oven to 200°c.

Put the sweet potato wedges into a roasting tin, drizzle with oil and season with a little salt and pepper. Roast in the oven for 20 minutes until crispy on the outside and soft in the middle.

Meanwhile, put the chorizo in a frying pan and fry for about 5 minutes until slightly crispy, and then add the tomatoes. Cook for another 3 to 4 minutes until the tomatoes are softened.

Meanwhile, put a large pan of water on to boil with a splash of white wine vinegar for the poached eggs. Poach the eggs to your liking (we find that 3 minutes is perfect).

Halve the avocado and scoop the flesh out into a bowl. Add a squeeze of lemon juice, some salt and pepper and a splash of Tabasco sauce. Mash together.

When the eggs are ready, plate everything up and drizzle the chorizo cooking oils over the eggs.

Preparation time: 10 minutes | Cooking time: 20 minutes | Serves: 2

A MOMENT OF INDULGENCE

HOMEMADE MARMALADES, CHUTNEYS, JAMS AND JELLIES MADE WITH A HINT OF SPICE!

Kanwal inherited her passion for food from her mother while growing up in the Punjab region of India. She went on to learn how to blend delicate spices in cookery school, before moving to England in 1978. Since then Kanwal has run numerous workshops and courses teaching traditional ways to cook Indian dishes, sharing her own recipes with her students. In the 1990s she presented a cookery show on Indian Sky channel Namaste.

In 2014 Kanwal decided to establish her own range of artisan food products, and so Hibiscus Lily was born. With Indian-inspired cuisine at its heart, Kanwal's range of delicious chutneys, relishes, marmalades, jams, jellies and spiced nuts are all produced by hand in Hitchin. Everything is made using traditional methods and natural ingredients without the use of additives or artificial preservatives (three relishes have no added sugar too).

Let's start at the breakfast table. If you are a marmalade-lover, try the ruby grapefruit with hibiscus and ginger marmalade on your toast, or perhaps the Seville orange marmalade with a hint of cinnamon and saffron.

To liven up your lunches, tomato with mango and apricot relish or beetroot and rhubarb chutney would be delicious with cheeses or cold meats. You can also use Hibiscus Lily's chutneys to make marinades and salad dressings: an easy way to add flavour and glaze. Use date and tamarind chutney, for example, to spice up strips of chicken (just mix together and stir, fry or bake), or why not make a carrot cake with it (see over the page)?

For anyone who has a taste for chillies, try the sumptuous hot chilli jam or flavoursome no added sugar relishes, chilli and tomato relish or chilli with roasted garlic relish.

Kanwal has won numerous national awards for her preserves including Gold in The World's Original Marmalade Awards and a Great Taste Award in 2017 for her popular lemon and ginger with turmeric marmalade; it can be used in a sweet or savoury way whether on toast and crumpets, with a cheeseboard or to glaze meat. The jellies include pomegranate with rose petals and hibiscus and pomegranate which received a Great Taste Award in 2018 (do try them made into drinks).

If you would like to try Hibiscus Lily preserves, jellies and spiced nuts, head to The Little Deli in Hitchin, Hertford Town and Tourist Info, Nourish Wholefood Café in Letchworth Garden City and Smallford Farm Shop just outside St Albans.

CARROT CAKE WITH A TWIST

Our easy recipe brings carrot cake to life and every bite is full of spice and flavours from Hibiscus Lily Date & Tamarind Chutney. Tamarind creates a carrot cake that is rich yet light and keeps the cake moist for longer.

200g light brown sugar

150ml sunflower oil

3 medium eggs, beaten

200g self-raising flour

1 tsp ground cinnamon

1 tsp bicarbonate of soda

150g Hibiscus Lily Date and Tamarind Chutney

150g carrots, peeled and grated

50g dried cranberries

50g golden raisins

TOPPING (OPTIONAL)

200g cream cheese, room temperature

90g salted butter, room temperature

400-450g icing sugar

1 tsp vanilla extract

Preheat the oven to 180°c, or 160°c for fan ovens.

In a large bowl, mix the sugar and oil well. Pour the beaten eggs onto the sugar mix and lightly mix with a spoon.

Sieve together the flour, cinnamon and bicarbonate of soda in a separate bowl.

In a mini blender, blend the chutney to a smooth paste and then stir into the sugar and egg mixture. Stir in the grated carrots.

Add the cranberries and golden raisins to the dry ingredients and then add it to the wet mix. Stir well with a spoon.

Pour the cake batter into a 20 to 22cm (8 to 9 inch) cake tin and bake for 35 to 45 minutes. Check after 35 minutes as ovens do vary. The cake should be well risen and springy; check with a skewer or knife inserted to make sure it's cooked inside. When cooked, turn out onto a wire rack.

The delicious cake can be eaten as it is or with a topping made as follows.

Mix the cream cheese and butter in a large mixer bowl and beat until smooth. Add half the icing sugar and vanilla extract and mix well. Add the remaining icing sugar and mix until smooth. Spread over the cooled cake to serve.

Preparation time: 20 minutes | Cooking time: 35-45 minutes | Serves: 9

STYLE AND SUBSTANCE

PRETTY WELWYN VILLAGE IS A LOVELY PLACE TO EXPLORE, AND IS FULL OF INTERESTING, INDEPENDENT FOOD BUSINESSES; IF A CUP OF TEA AND A DELICIOUS SLICE OF CAKE IS YOUR THING, LOOK NO FURTHER!

If you stroll through Welwyn Village you will spot Laura Kate, a stylish tea shop which is noticeable from the cake stands and cakes in the window. The charming building with its sash windows is beautifully decorated inside and out, with a crisp white frontage, silver wallpaper, vintage-style furnishings and fresh flowers. It is positively the perfect place to stop for morning coffee, a spot of lunch or full afternoon tea.

The cakes and bakes in the counter are all homemade which is a rarity in this day and age. Everything is made in the shop by the small team, and the display of cupcakes, slices and bakes change daily. Favourite flavours include classic Victoria Sponge, Lemon Meringue, Salted Caramel and Raspberry Cheesecake to name a few. For those who prefer a savoury option you can also order toasted crumpets, English muffins and cheese scones, as well paninis and sandwiches for something more substantial.

The tea shop is table service, rather than queue-up, which creates a relaxed feel. Afternoon tea is very popular and small groups often book in for special birthdays, baby showers or just to get friends together. Start with fresh finger sandwiches, then move onto warm scones with clotted cream, raspberry compote or lemon curd, then finish with petit fours, macarons and mini cakes. Everything is made freshly to order and therefore any dietary requirements such as coeliac or vegan can be easily accommodated.

Tea is the focus at Laura Kate, all of it being loose leaf. It is served in pretty vintage-style teapots and cups. The variety includes Ceylon, Rooibos, Earl Grey, Darjeeling, White Tea and Chamomile as well as classic English Breakfast which can also be ordered as decaffeinated.

Laura Kate has been nominated for many local awards, including the Hertfordshire Life Food & Drink Award for Best Independent Café/Tea Room.

SNICKERLICIOUS CHOCOLATE CAKE

This cake is a favourite with Laura Kate customers. It was created by my husband, who always requests a slice when it is baked in the shop! It is an amazing combination of oozy caramel, decadent Nutella and rich peanut butter… Snickerlicious!

FOR THE SPONGE

350g plain flour

200g cocoa powder, plus extra for dusting

1 tsp salt

2 tsp bicarbonate of soda

200g margarine, plus extra for greasing

400g granulated sugar

140g light brown sugar

4 eggs

480ml milk

FOR THE PEANUT BUTTER BUTTERCREAM

500g butter

1kg icing sugar

4 tbsp peanut butter

Dash of milk

FOR THE CHOCOLATE TOPPING

150g dark or milk chocolate

1 Snickers bar, chopped

FOR THE FILLING

420g jar of Nutella

400g Carnation caramel

Preheat the oven to 190°c (170°c fan). Grease two 20cm round baking tins with a little margarine and lightly dust with cocoa.

FOR THE SPONGE

Put the flour, cocoa, salt and bicarbonate of soda into a mixing bowl.

Put the margarine and sugars in a separate bowl. Beat for 3 minutes with an electric whisk on medium to high speed until softened. Add the eggs one at a time and beat on a medium speed after each addition.

Add the flour mixture in three batches, alternating with the milk. Beat on a medium speed.

Run a spatula around the bowl to make sure everything is well mixed. Divide the mixture equally between the prepared tins. Bake for 45 minutes in a preheated oven or until a skewer inserted into the centre of the cakes comes out clean. Remove from the oven and run a knife around the inside of the cake tin.

Leave for 5 minutes before turning out onto a wire rack to cool.

FOR THE PEANUT BUTTER BUTTERCREAM

Place the butter in a mixing bowl and beat on a medium speed until smooth. Add the icing sugar and peanut butter and beat for 3 minutes on high speed. Add a dash of milk to soften. Beat for 3 minutes on high speed until smooth and fluffy.

FOR THE CHOCOLATE TOPPING

Place the chocolate in a microwaveable dish and melt in 30 second intervals in the microwave, stirring between each 30 seconds until melted.

FOR THE FILLING

When the cake is cooled, slice each cake in half. Spread a thick layer of Nutella on one half. Spread a thick layer of caramel on one half then spread a thick layer of peanut butter buttercream on the third half. Sandwich together.

TO FINISH

Add a generous layer of buttercream around the top and outside of the cake. Then chill for 1 hour. Once chilled pour the melted chocolate slowly on top of the cake and coax it towards the edges, letting it drip down the side. Pipe some remaining buttercream in swirls on the top. Decorate with the chopped Snickers bar.

Preparation time: 25 minutes | Cooking time: 45 minutes | Serves 10-15 (depending on how large the slices are!)

DELICIOUS & SUSTAINABLE

Anyone from Hertfordshire who loves food knows about Lussmanns Sustainable Fish & Grill Restaurants. After opening their first venue in Hertford back in 2004, Lussmanns has grown organically as more people discover its delicious, affordable food and eco-credentials.

Owner Andrei Lussmann has always done things a little differently. Before it became trendy, he cared about sourcing and seasonality and his menus have always reflected that. They specialise in fish, and are, at the time of writing, the only restaurant group in the UK to have a fully MSC certified wild fish menu. With a rotating fish list which includes haddock, cod cheeks and hake, Lussmanns was also the first restaurant to serve MSC monkfish and ling supplied by Hertfordshire-based company The Stickleback Fish Company, while their signature fishcake with spinach, caper and parsley butter sauce has been on the menu from the start.

As well as all that, Lussmanns has always worked closely with artisan producers and the best organic suppliers they can find. Beef, lamb and pork are all organically reared, while their chicken is Heritage Label Anglais. Puds have a British-feel too, with honey and thyme pudding and Bramley apple and hazelnut crumble regulars on the menu. Responsible sourcing continues into the drinks with Luscombe organic juices and a wide range of British beers on offer, many sourced within close proximity to the restaurants.

Andrei says: "we want to show people that sustainable doesn't mean expensive and that you can eat out really well and affordably knowing that the food has been ethically sourced."

Andrei also has an eye for amazing locations and each Lussmanns is in the centre of its community, in quirky, atmospheric buildings that make eating out a real experience. The Egyptian house in Hertford has a fantastic exterior, with the Egypt-inspired carvings picked out in gold, while their Hitchin restaurant is in a Grade II-listed building just off the bustling Market Square. A grand former bank is now the home of Lussmanns Tring, while Harpenden is an 18th century former coach house within a charming walled garden filled with flowers. The St Albans restaurant is a modern contemporary glass and sleek steel building with bird's-eye views over The Vintry Garden.

Despite their beautiful surroundings and high-end feel, eating in the restaurants is good value for money as part of the Lussmanns ethos. They always have a great set menu which runs from 12 to 7pm, and if it's a special occasion, you can reserve one of the private dining rooms. Lussmanns has been recognised nationally too; with Giles Coren named them as one of his favourite restaurants in The Times Top 100 Restaurants, and they have also won many awards, most recently 'Menu of the Year' from the Marine Stewardship Council (2019) and Source Fish Responsibly Award from Food Made Good (2018).

SIGNATURE FISHCAKES

Our signature fishcakes have been on our menu since we first opened and remain as popular today as then: we wouldn't be allowed to take them off! We use MSC hake and smoked haddock in our fishcakes, served simply with baby spinach and a parsley butter sauce but you could serve with steamed vegetables or salad, if you prefer.

700g Maris Piper potatoes, peeled and chopped

250g MSC hake fillet, skinned and diced (or any MSC white fish)

250g MSC smoked haddock fillet, skinned and diced

Wedge of lemon

Small bunch of coriander, washed and chopped

Freshly ground black pepper and salt

150g breadcrumbs (ideally panko)

3 eggs

500ml vegetable oil, for frying

First, cook the potatoes by steaming or boiling for 10 to 15 minutes until softened.

Place the hake and haddock in a bowl and mix together. Place in a large pan with the wedge of lemon and cover with water. Heat until the water starts to simmer, then drain the fish using a colander and set aside to cool. Remove the lemon wedge.

Place the potato in a large bowl and mash well. Add the coriander and mix into the mash. Add the fish mix to the mash and mix well, adding salt and pepper to taste. Set to one side.

Crack the eggs into a bowl and beat together. Place the breadcrumbs in another bowl.

Take about a sixth of the fishcake mix and roll into a ball, then flatten slightly into a patty shape.

Place the fishcake in the egg and then in the breadcrumbs, coating well, and patting off any excess breadcrumbs. Repeat to make the remaining fishcakes.

Put the vegetable oil into a heavy-bottomed pan and heat. Test with a few breadcrumbs dropped in the oil; once they bubble the oil is ready.

Turn down the heat a little and fry each fishcake until they are golden brown. Serve with your choice of vegetables or salad.

Preparation time: 15 minutes | Cooking time: 25-30 minutes | Makes 6 fishcakes

PRIDE OF HERTS

RIGHT AT THE HEART OF HERTFORD, THE MCMULLENS BREWERY AND PUBS ARE KNOWN ACROSS THE COUNTY, AND WHEREVER YOU ARE, WHETHER IN A TOWN OR VILLAGE, THERE WILL BE ONE WITHIN WALKING DISTANCE!

Located on the River Lea in Hertford, McMullens has a very long history of brewing; Peter McMullen took over in 1827 and since then the family have brewed in Hertford without a break. They still use water drawn from the McMullen well, and the beers are sent all across Hertfordshire and beyond. McMullens have protected the company's brewing history throughout that time by acquiring and investing in public houses and many of the pubs date back hundreds of years, such as The Woolpack, which has a brewing history dating back to 1743; you can even moor outside! You will spot their pubs right across Hertfordshire, including Hitchin, Royston, Potters Bar and St Albans as well as in many villages. The pubs are often run by managers or business partners, allowing them to showcase their own culinary skills and listen to customers.

Located just outside Sawbridgeworth, The Orange Tree has been a pub since 1901 and is now run by chef Gareth Davies. It has an excellent reputation for food, drawing customers from far and wide, and everything is made at the pub, following Gareth's own recipes. As Gareth explains, "we like to serve predominantly British dishes with a few plates from my Michelin days. We source the best ingredients we can from within 20 miles of the pub and pride ourselves on the service we give." They have a daily changing specials board which features fresh fish caught from UK day boats, and they make daily trips to the butchers, so there is always something new to try at The Orange Tree. Plus the garden is lovely in the summer, so well worth a trip out to the Hertfordshire countryside.

Right at the edges of Hertfordshire (the canal marks the border!) The Dusty Miller is another jewel in the McMullen's crown, with outstanding food from chef Chris Cleary, who used to work at Coq d'argent in Bank and The Old Bull and Bush in Hampstead. The team use many local suppliers, including Bridget B's meats, eggs from East End Farm in Roydon, fish from Stickleback in Potters Bar and Dawlicious ice cream from Hertford Heath.

The Orange Tree
Herb Garden

SHEPHERD'S PIE

We change the menu with the seasons at The Orange Tree, and this is one of our winter favourites, which we serve with leeks and turnips. It is strong on flavour but very simple to execute. Perfect comfort food!

200ml milk

200ml double cream

500g Maris Piper potatoes, peeled and chopped

200g salted butter

Rapeseed oil, for frying

500g lamb mince, the best you can find

125ml white wine

500g heritage carrots, diced

250g banana shallots, diced

125g celery, diced

125ml lamb stock (you can buy this from any good supermarket)

2 sprigs of thyme

2 tbsp Heinz tomato ketchup

1 tbsp Worcestershire sauce

2 egg yolks

Freshly ground black pepper and sea salt

Put the milk and cream in a large pan and bring to the boil, then drop in the potatoes. Cook for 15 minutes or until the potatoes are tender (be careful the mixture doesn't boil over the pan).

Drain the potatoes and add the butter. Mash the potatoes until all the lumps are removed, then season with salt to your taste. Leave in the pan as you'll come back to this later.

Heat a large frying pan and add the oil; heat until it's quite hot. Add the lamb and cook for about 5 minutes until it's nice and brown.

Drain off any excess fat and liquid.

Place the pan over a shallow heat and add the white wine. Heat until the wine has reduced by half then add the carrots, shallots and celery and simmer for about 4 minutes until they are softened but still crunchy.

Add the lamb stock, stir, and then simmer until the meat has absorbed most of the liquid. You can add more stock if the pie mix is a little dry. Add the thyme, ketchup and Worcestershire sauce and season to taste with salt and pepper.

Preheat the oven to 200°c.

Place the mixture into a serving dish and set aside for a few minutes. Mix the two egg yolks into the mash (this will give the mash a lovely shine/gloss finish). Spoon the mash into a piping bag and pipe the mash on top of the pie mix until completely covered. If you haven't got a piping bag, place the mash on top of the lamb mixture evenly, then spread it out with the back of a spoon.

Place the pie in the oven and cook until the mash has gone golden brown and is bubbling, which will take about 30 minutes.

Preparation time: 15 minutes | Cooking time: 55 minutes | Serves 4

PAN-ROASTED SEA TROUT, CREAMED CAULIFLOWER, POTATO TERRINE, ROASTED ROOT VEGETABLES AND CRISPY KALE

This dish is very versatile and you can use whichever fish is in season; just ask your fishmonger for recommendations. You can also vary the vegetables to the seasons, so it works well in the winter and the summer.

4 x 200g sea trout fillets (salmon will work just as well)

Sea salt and freshly ground black pepper

FOR THE POTATO TERRINE

75g butter, melted

10 Maris Piper potatoes, peeled and sliced using a mandoline

Parmesan, grated

FOR THE CRISPY KALE

200g curly kale, stripped from the stalks, stalks discarded

4 tbsp rapeseed oil

FOR THE ROASTED VEGETABLES

½ swede

3 turnips

½ celeriac

2 carrots, medium

1 parsnip

75ml olive oil

FOR THE CREAMED CAULIFLOWER

25g butter

1 medium Maris Piper potato, peeled and diced

1 small cauliflower, cut into small florets

200ml full-fat milk

100ml double cream

Preheat the oven to 180°c.

FOR THE POTATO TERRINE

Brush the bottom and sides of a medium-sized baking dish with the melted butter and then start to layer the potato slices. Between each layer, brush over melted butter, then sprinkle with parmesan, salt and pepper. Finish with a final layer of potato brushed generously with butter. Cover the top with foil and cook in the oven for 1 hour 30 minutes or until potatoes are tender throughout. Remove from the oven. In the pub we make this terrine the night before, cut into slices, and then fry in a dry, non-stick pan until golden and crispy to serve, but you can serve it straight from the baking tray.

FOR THE CRISPY KALE

Mix the kale with the rapeseed oil and a good pinch of salt in a large bowl, so that all the leaves are coated. Spread the leaves on a baking tray and place in the oven for 25 minutes, turning once midway through. Set aside once cooked.

FOR THE ROASTED VEGETABLES

Peel all the vegetables and cut into similar sized pieces. Put a large pan of water on to boil, then par-boil the vegetables, starting with the carrot, then 5 minutes later add the celeriac followed by the remaining veg. Cook until just softened. Place the vegetables on a large roasting tray (do not overcrowd). Drizzle with olive oil and roast for about 15 minutes.

FOR THE CREAMED CAULIFLOWER

Make this while the vegetables are in the oven. Melt the butter in a large pan over a low heat. Add the cauliflower florets and potato then cook for 2 to 3 minutes, stirring regularly until they begin to colour.

Add the milk and cream, season well with salt and bring to the boil. Cover with a lid and simmer gently for 8 to 12 minutes, depending on their size, or until the cauliflower is really soft.

Blend everything with a hand blender, then pass through a sieve and season.

When the potato terrine has about 10 minutes to go, cook the fish. Preheat a non-stick pan. Season the trout fillets and place in the pan skin-side down. To stop the fish curling, press lightly with a fish slice. Depending on thickness, cook for 3 to 5 minutes until you have a crispy skin.

When the potato terrine is ready, check that everything is hot and plate up, as shown in the photograph.

Preparation time: 45 minutes | Cooking time: 1 hour 40 minutes | Serves 4

SEARED SCALLOPS, SWEETCORN PURÉE, CHARRED SWEETCORN & CHORIZO JAM

Scallops are always popular at the Dusty Miller and we are always trying out new and exciting ways to put them on the menu, often using ingredients you will already have in your kitchen. The recipe came about from being on a ski lift in Norway thinking about what the new scallop dish would be when we came back.

FOR THE CHORIZO JAM

1 tsp rapeseed or olive oil

1 red onion, finely diced

100g chorizo, finely diced

1 clove of garlic, minced

¼ tsp chopped fresh rosemary

¼ tsp chopped fresh thyme

1 tbsp tomato purée

150ml apple juice

1 tbsp dark muscovado sugar

1 tsp balsamic vinegar

½ tsp soy sauce

FOR THE SWEETCORN PURÉE

100g unsalted butter

1 banana shallot, peeled and chopped

2 cloves of garlic, crushed

300g sweetcorn kernels (frozen or fresh)

6 pinches of Maldon sea salt

150ml double cream

FOR THE CHARRED SWEETCORN

1 corn on the cob, husked

FOR THE SCALLOPS

12 scallops

Rapeseed or olive oil

Knob of butter

¼ lemon, to squeeze

Micro herbs, to garnish

FOR THE CHORIZO JAM

Using a small saucepan over a medium heat, add the oil, followed by the onion and chorizo. Cook, stirring every few minutes, until the onions are translucent.

Add the garlic, rosemary and thyme. Continue cooking for a further 2 minutes.

Add the remaining ingredients and bring the pan to a gentle simmer until the mixture has reduced and the consistency thickens. Pour into a jar and seal. Once cool the jam can be stored for 14 days in the fridge.

FOR THE SWEETCORN PURÉE

Put the butter in a saucepan and heat until melted then add the shallot, garlic and sweetcorn. Cook over a gentle heat until the shallot is softened and translucent. Season well with the Maldon sea salt, add the double cream and cook until the sweetcorn is soft. Purée in a blender and then pass through a fine sieve.

FOR THE CHARRED SWEETCORN

Bring a pan of water to the boil and place the corn in. Cook for 8 to 10 minutes. Drain. If you have a blow torch, char the corn, then slice off 12 sections of the kernels. You can also grill the corn to give it colour, before slicing off the kernels. Set aside.

FOR THE SCALLOPS

Clean the scallops by washing under cold water. Remove the skirt and orange coral. Dry on kitchen paper. Heat a frying pan until very hot. Add a little oil, season the scallops with salt and pepper and cook for 1 minute on each side until golden brown. Finish with a knob of butter and a squeeze of lemon.

When everything is ready, reheat the purée if you need to, then start by creating a pattern of sweetcorn purée across four plates. Place three scallops as you like. Place the charred corn each side and intermittently garnish with the chorizo jam. Finish with micro herbs of your choice.

Preparation time: 15 minutes | Cooking time: 45 minutes | Serves 4

A PERFECT COMBINATION

FEATURING BOWLS PILED WITH DELICIOUS SALADS, AND A WINDOW FILLED WITH CAKES, PARKER & VINE IS THE HERTSFORDSHIRE VERSION OF OTTOLENGHI!

Jane Parker and Sue Vine opened their stylish deli in Harpenden just a couple of years ago, and their attractive salads, handmade cakes, coffee and useful deli ingredients have been a big hit.

You may also know Parker & Vine from events at Childwickbury, the Hospice of St Francis garden party at Ashridge, and other food festivals around Hertfordshire, where their salads and cakes always draw queues.

Generous piles of vegetables, handfuls of herbs and delicious spices combine to make the beautiful salads you see in colourful dishes on the counter. Slices of roasted aubergine with pomegranate seeds; roasted butternut squash with couscous, almonds and dried apricots; superfood salad with broccoli, sprouting beans, pumpkin seeds, mint and feta... you can choose a boxful to take away for lunch or order a whole dish for parties. Choose a thick slice of kiln-roasted honey glazed salmon, kofte or vegetarian quiche to go with and that's an easy supper sorted!

Shelves line the walls with interesting indie products, including Sarah & Finn's preserves, Cool Chile's ketchups and Beanworks' coffee beans. Parker & Vine also stock a wide range of Middle Eastern cooking ingredients.

If you are feeding a crowd, the team can make a large tray or two of something delicious to take away, such as slow-roast lamb shoulder with mahgreb spices, beef bourguignon or griddled za'atar chicken, as well as meze platters: all perfect for sharing, whatever the occasion.

Creative and seasonal baking is at the heart of what they do, and the window display is always enticing, with chocolate cakes piled with chocolate buttons and flakes, buttery flapjacks, sticky lemon cakes and more, all sold either whole or by slice. Their Christmas cakes and mince pies are in high demand each year and you can also get traditional Easter bakes such as Simnel cakes and hot cross buns. During The Great British Bake Off, the team recreate the technical bakes for fun, so you can take them home to eat while watching!

Sustainability is an issue Parker & Vine take seriously, and they took the decision last year to stop providing single-use cups for takeaway coffee and tea. Customers are gently encouraged to bring in their own reusable cups or 'rent' one from the shop, and the idea has caught on.

ROAST CAULIFLOWER WITH POMEGRANATE SEEDS, SPRING ONION AND GREEN TAHINI DRESSING

You are in for a revelation if you haven't ever roasted a cauliflower! Tahini is a Middle Eastern dressing made from sesame seed paste – confusingly also called tahini – so try to find a brand from the Middle East rather than Europe; Lebanese brands are considered best.
Serve this salad warm or at ambient temperature; it makes a fantastic accompaniment to either meat or fish or served as part of a vegetarian or vegan sharing platter.

I large (or 2 small) fresh cauliflower

50g extra-virgin olive oil

Salt

Freshly ground black pepper

Baby spinach leaves

1-2 pomegranates, seeds only

1 bunch of spring onions, finely sliced

2-3 green chilies, finely sliced

FOR THE GREEN TAHINI DRESSING

150g tahini paste

150ml water

1 clove of garlic, crushed

2 tbsp lemon juice

¼ tsp salt, or more, to taste

Handful of fresh flat-leaf parsley leaves

Preheat the oven to 190°c.

Break or cut the cauliflower into florets (you can use the stalks and any fresh leaves too) and cut any large florets in half. Toss the cauliflower in the olive oil to coat generously. Season with salt and pepper.

Line one or two baking trays with baking parchment and spread the cauliflower out on the trays leaving space between the florets for the hot air to circulate. Roast for 30 to 40 minutes, turning halfway through. When cooked a knife will pierce the cauliflower easily and the cauliflower will be lightly caramelised. Set aside to cool while you make the dressing.

Put the tahini paste, garlic, lemon juice and salt into a food processor or blender and whizz. Slowly add water until you have the consistency of double cream; the amount of water specified is a guide only.

Taste and adjust the seasoning; your tahini dressing may taste a little harsh or bitter at first, and if this is the case, counterintuitively what you need to add is salt to take away the bitterness. You can also add more lemon juice or garlic if desired.

Add the parsley leaves and give the dressing a final blitz. (You can make the sauce in a bowl using a hand whisk but a machine gives the dressing a lovely creaminess.)

To assemble the dish, place a layer of spinach leaves on the bottom of your serving platter followed by a generous layer of the roast cauliflower. Spoon over the green tahini dressing leaving some of the cauliflower showing. Sprinkle with some pomegranate seeds, spring onion and green chilli then repeat the layers until all the cauliflower is used up.

NOTE: The tahini dressing will keep for up to 4 days in the fridge, though it will thicken with time and you may need to let down again with a little water.

FARM FRESH

SURROUNDED BY FIELDS, THIS WELCOMING CAFÉ AND FARM SHOP JUST OFF THE BUSY A10 IS POPULAR ALL YEAR, WHETHER YOU GO TO PICK-YOUR-OWN STRAWBERRIES, BUY LOCALLY SOURCED PRODUCTS OR FOR AFTERNOON TEA ON THE TERRACE.

Family-run Pearce's Farm Shop and Café is easy to find between Puckeridge and Buntingford and draws customers from all over Hertfordshire and beyond. The Pearces started farming in the early 80s and sold their fruit and vegetables from a shed on the field. The farm shop has grown considerably since then but the same passion for excellent food continues, whether you buy seasonal produce to take home or stay for lunch in the bright, spacious café.

Pick-your-own in the summer is popular and their strawberries and raspberries are also made into preserves (using Granny Pearce's original recipes) which are available from the shop. Their asparagus is a highlight in late spring and you can buy an amazing selection of root veg, beets and pumpkins in the autumn.

The shop has become a showcase for the finest local producers including bread from Simmons, tea from Ware-based Tealicious, and the coffee is sourced and hand roasted by White House in neighbouring Manuden and also used in the café. Fresh meats are sourced locally and there is a great range of cooked meats and fish too. An abundance of pastas, grains and store cupboard ingredients will fill your basket along with

eggs, yoghurt and British cheeses. The deli section (much of it homemade) includes quiches, pies, salads, hummus and more. A fine selection of wines, local gins, beers and soft drinks will complete your meal.

The café has an excellent local reputation earning it many awards as well as inclusion in the Waitrose Good Food Guide (so do book a table). Pearce's use their own-grown produce, so you'll spot asparagus during spring and soups and roasted vegetables during colder months. Served by friendly waiting staff, lunch offers weekly seasonal specials alongside popular classics with dishes such as crispy duck salad, fish and chips or Sri Lankan curry as well as sandwiches and wraps. Roast Sunday lunches with all the trimmings attract the crowds. Afternoon teas are served on three-tier stands, with finger sandwiches, savouries, freshly baked cakes, pastries and warm homemade scones with jam and clotted cream. But if you just want to pop in for a coffee or a gin and tonic, that's fine too!

"We take great pride," says Ed Pearce, "in providing the best quality produce and delicious home-cooked food, and work hard to ensure our customers really enjoy their visit."

OUR OWN ASPARAGUS WITH CRUSHED POTATO, BACON, POACHED EGG AND HOLLANDAISE SAUCE

English asparagus has the most wonderful flavour and is the best in the world! We grow it here on the farm; it is a labour of love though as each spear grows fast, up to 15 centimetres a day, and has to be harvested by hand when it reaches the right height. The growing season from mid-April is only about 8 weeks, so do look out for when the bunches are available. Our chef likes to char-grill the asparagus which adds a lovely smoky flavour to this dish, one that is always popular in the café.

FOR THE CRUSHED POTATOES

500g cooked new potatoes
Olive oil
2 shallots, finely chopped
1 clove of garlic, crushed
Small bunch of chives, chopped

FOR THE ASPARAGUS

2 bunches of asparagus, ends trimmed
Olive oil
Freshly ground black pepper and sea salt

FOR THE HOLLANDAISE SAUCE

3 egg yolks
3 tbsp white wine vinegar
250g unsalted butter, melted
Hot water

FOR THE POACHED EGGS

4 eggs
2 litres water
500ml clear vinegar
Bowl of iced water

TO SERVE

120g cooked bacon, chopped
Sprigs of parsley or pea shoots

FOR THE CRUSHED POTATOES

To make the crushed potatoes, heat a little olive oil in a pan and cook the shallots and garlic for about 10 minutes until soft. Add the potatoes and crush with a fork. Stir until warmed through then stir in the chives.

FOR THE ASPARAGUS

Meanwhile, toss the asparagus in a little olive oil and season. Grill for about 3 to 5 minutes (depending on how thick they are), turning often, until tender when tested with a fork.

FOR THE HOLLANDAISE SAUCE

To make the hollandaise sauce, bring a half-filled saucepan of water to the boil and place a heatproof mixing bowl over it. Turn the heat as low as possible to just keep the water simmering. Put the egg yolks and vinegar in the bowl and using a balloon whisk, whisk until thick and creamy. Continuing to whisk slowly, add the melted butter with 50ml hot water until the butter has been incorporated and you have a lovely smooth, thick sauce. Season to taste.

FOR THE POACHED EGGS

In another pan, make the poached eggs. Bring the water and vinegar to the boil in a pan then reduce to a simmer. Crack the eggs one at a time into a small bowl and gently tip into the simmering water. Poach the eggs for 3½ minutes then remove with a slotted spoon and gently place in the iced water to stop the cooking.

TO SERVE

When ready to serve, place a spoonful of crushed potato on a plate, followed by the asparagus spears. Spoon over the hollandaise sauce, scatter over the cooked bacon and top with a poached egg and sprig of parsley or pea shoots.

Preparation time: 20 minutes | Cooking time: 20 minutes | Serves 4

FOR EVERYONE

CUSTOMERS RETURN TIME AND AGAIN TO PER TUTTI FOR THEIR WARM
WELCOME, HOSPITALITY AND DELICIOUS ITALIAN FOOD

'Per Tutti' means 'for everyone' in Italian, and it is the perfect name for these family-run Italian restaurants in Berkhamstead and St Albans. At any time of the day or evening you will find the restaurants packed with regulars, and everyone is welcome, from babies to business people. Olga is in charge of front of house and her energy sets the atmosphere for the restaurants. As she says, they "are not about tablecloths"; Per Tutti is for everyday, affordable dining. The vibe is modern, with fun decor including a red Fiat that takes up a whole wall in the St Albans venue.

Olga's partner Jovan is the head chef and he and his teams work incredibly hard to keep everyone happy with classic Italian dishes such as pasta, pizza, grilled fish, steaks and chicken. All their pasta is hand-made and if you want gluten-free, they can make that for you. If you are craving a really great spaghetti bolognese or lasagne, you will be happy here, and if you want to ring the changes, try the melanzane cannelloni or the fettuccine pesto rosso, made with peppers, mushrooms, broccoli and red pesto. The most popular dish on the menu is the linguine di mare, made with tiger prawns, clams, squid and mussels in a white wine sauce and people come from all over Hertfordshire to order this dish.

Per Tutti St Albans only opened a few years ago, just near the entrance to the Cathedral on Holywell Hill, and it has already made an impact locally, winning recognition for Best Everyday and most Family Friendly restaurant. Olga and Jovan had to extend into the building next door after a year, and then opened another room and it's still tricky to get a table at the weekend! They opened in neighbouring Berkhamstead in 2018 and already have regulars who come in each week. Brothers Leo and Besi run Per Tutti in Berkhamstead and know many customers by name.

Save space for the great puds, which are suitably Italian, with homemade tiramisu and lemon, lime and honey cake, as well as affogato (vanilla gelato with crushed biscotti, served with a shot of espresso and amaretto liqueur), and a delicious range of gelato and sorbet. A scoop of hazelnut gelato is lovely at any time of the year; why wait for summer?

PER TUTTi

LINGUINE DI MARE

This very popular Italian dish translates to 'fruits of the sea' and has been a bestseller at Per Tutti since day one. Customers have mentioned that it brings back memories of holiday in Italy. So if they can't make it there on holiday they can come to us!

200g San Marzano pelati (whole plum tomatoes)

¼ large white onion, finely chopped

Freshly ground black pepper and salt, to taste

50ml extra-virgin olive oil, plus extra for cooking

Bunch of fresh basil, chopped

500g Dececco pasta linguine

1 clove of garlic, finely chopped

28 mussels, shell on

12 tiger prawns, peeled

4 king prawns, shell on and butterflied (cut open)

16 sliced rings of squid

28 vongole (clams), shelled

8 cherry tomatoes, cut in half

50ml white wine

Bunch of fresh parsley, chopped

To make the tomato sauce, put the tomatoes and onion in a saucepan, season with salt and pepper, and then simmer over a low heat for 1 hour. Meanwhile, cook the pasta according to the packet instructions until just al dente.

When ready, pour into a moulin, add the olive oil and work it through the moulin or mash until well combined. Stir in the chopped basil.

Heat a large frying pan, then add a slug of olive oil with the garlic and cook for 1 minute, then add all the fish (mussels, tiger and king prawns, squid and vongole), cherry tomatoes, white wine and half a ladle of the tomato sauce. Cook for 3 to 4 minutes while the sauce thickens then add the pasta and cook for a further few minutes (about 8 minutes in total). Season to taste with salt and pepper.

When ready to serve, put on one serving dish to share or divide between four dishes and garnish with chopped fresh parsley.

Preparation time: 15 minutes | Cooking time: 40 minutes | Serves 4

PERFECT PUDS

It was being a finalist on the first series of The Great British Bake Off that set Johnny Shepherd on his new path in life. For him, baking was about pudding, and coming from a family of bakers, he had been taught how to bake a great jam roly poly or treacle sponge. Too often he found puds in restaurants disappointing and nothing like the ones he knew from family gatherings and he felt sure others felt the same. "Why pudding? In most places pudding is disappointing, it's an afterthought. We wanted to do pudding properly. So we decided to just make pudding. That's it. We do one thing well," Johnny explains.

Johnny started with a Pudmobile parked outside St Albans train station. Tired, hungry and often-delayed commuters returning home love the tiny van packed with fresh doughnuts, custard tarts, Bakewell tarts and chocolate brownies. Word spread and two years later The Pudding Stop opened on Verulam Road and is now a busy café, serving home-baked goodies from morning until late at night. Find a spot on the long sharing tables and join in! The Pudmobile is still out and about and you can find it at many music and food festivals across Hertfordshire.

Everything you buy at the Pudmobile and in the café is baked right there in the café. Open seven days a week, you can go to the café for breakfast, where the menu focuses on their own pastries, cinnamon buns, buttermilk pancakes, brioche French toast and sourdough bagels. Bacon is sourced from a family farm in Suffolk where the pigs roam free and coffee is from Climpson & Sons.

By midday the bakers are busy filling doughnuts, baking brownies and blow-torching lemon meringue pies. And yes, you can get pudding for lunch! Sticky ginger pudding, chocolate chip and bread and butter pudding, Bramley apple crumble with proper vanilla custard, vegan chocolate cheesecake with hokey pokey... pudding is served until late and it's perfectly normal to go for dinner elsewhere and finish the night here. You can get pudding wine to go with your pud (of course), or an And Union beer or cocktail; marmalade martini anyone?

If you are having a party at home you can order a whole pud to serve 10 to 20 people; how about a whole treacle tart or a tray of salted caramel and peanut butter brownies? You can order 'Bake at Home' puds online for delivery anywhere in the UK and also buy them in the Selfridges Foodhall, but the heart of Pudding Stop will always be in St Albans, where it all started.

BAKED COOKIE DOUGH

This is the bestselling pud in our shop to eat in and take away. It's so popular that we have launched it in our Bake at Home range, and here it is for you to make yourself!

110g unsalted butter

85g light brown sugar

½ tsp sea salt flakes

½ tsp vanilla extract

1 egg, beaten

150g plain flour

½ tsp bicarbonate of soda

125g chocolate chips

Preheat the oven to 200°c.

Put the butter, sugar, salt and vanilla extract in a bowl, and mix together until softened.

Add the egg slowly and mix in. Sieve the flour and bicarbonate of soda together and add it gradually to the butter mixture. Stir in the chocolate chips.

Spoon the mixture evenly into four ramekins.

Bake for 10 to 15 minutes until firm at the edges but gooey in the middle!

Serve still warm with ice cream or cream.

Preparation time: 15 minutes | Cooking time: 40 minutes | Serves 4

SPIRIT OF THE OUTDOORS

UNDER STARS, BY A CAMPFIRE, A GIN WAS BORN, AND IS NOW SHARED ACROSS HERTFORDSHIRE AND BEYOND

Ben and Kate, founders of Puddingstone Distillery, settled on the name 'Campfire' for their core gin brand, recalling memorable times spent around campfires with warmth, food, conversation and a good gin and tonic in hand. Launched in 2016, Puddingstone Distillery has made a real impact on the local food and drins scene and beyond, most notably winning the World's Best Martini Challenge in 2019 for their Campfire London Dry Gin recipe.

The first gin distillery in Hertfordshire, Puddingstone is situated at the base of Wilstone Reservoir, just five minutes from Tring in the beautiful Chiltern Hills. There are four main gins in the core range: London Dry, Old Tom, Cask Aged and Navy Strength, all produced on two stills named after female adventurers, Isabella (Lucy Bird) and Amelia (Earhart). To date the Campfire Gin range carries an impressive seven international spirits awards and critical acclaim from drinks industry and national press.

Annually, Puddingstone Distillery release limited edition gins, including the recent 1594 Spirit of Box Moor, distilled with rare, Hertfordshire-grown juniper. Campfire Special Edition No 1 is another gin they are very proud of; 'a pink gin with a purpose' made with Himalayan balsam flowers from sites managed by the Herts & Middlesex Wildlife Trust, this gin has now raised over £5K for the trust and has featured on BBC News, ITV Anglia News and The One Show.

You can buy the gins in their own distillery shop on Fridays and Saturdays, by appointment at other times or from the website. You will also spot the distinctive bottles on the shelves of many local shops, including Pearce's Farm Shop in Buntingford, F L Dickins in Rickmansworth, Tomoka Spirits Boutique, The Fleetville Larder in St Albans and the Hertford Tourist Information Centre. It is also on the bar at The Grove Hotel in Watford, The Akeman in Tring, Dylans in St Albans, The Rising Sun in Berkhamsted and at Crocker's in Tring where they collaborated on a unique gin for the restaurant.

Cocktail demos and food pairing events in the distillery are also chances to work with other local indies; Toby Murray from Beechwoods in Tring (a world cheese judge) co-hosts the gin and cheese tasting events, and Mat Leaver from Curious Foods co-hosts the charcuterie events. Next up are chocolate pairings with Yvette's Chocolates.

CAMPFIRE BONE DRY MARTINI

Here's our World's Best Martini Challenge 2019 winning martini recipe.

*10 parts Campfire London Dry Gin
(room temperature)*

*1 part Dolin Dry Vermouth
(fridge temperature)*

*Orange peel flower garnishes soaked in
Carpano Antica Formula rosso vermouth
for 10 hours*

Ice for dilution

Combine the gin and vermouth with ice and stir; you are aiming for dilution equaling two and a half parts water. Serve in a chilled glass and garnish with the orange peel flowers.

BALSAMIC AND CHERRY SHRUB

FOR THE BALSAMIC AND CHERRY SHRUB

400g cherries, stoned

420g light brown muscovado sugar

10 black peppercorns, cracked

225ml balsamic vinegar

TO MAKE

25ml balsamic and cherry shrub

75ml Campfire Navy Strength Gin

100ml Fever-Tree Indian tonic

FOR THE BALSAMIC AND CHERRY SHRUB

Add the cherries, sugar and peppercorns to a bowl and mix well. Cover and put in the fridge for 24 hours. Strain and add vinegar to taste.

TO MAKE

Add the shrub and gin to a shaker filled with ice. Stir, strain into a glass and add tonic.

Preparation time: 5 minutes, plus 24 hours for the shrub | Serves 1

PERFECT POLISH

HERTFORDSHIRE-BASED FOOD WRITER REN BEHAN HAS WRITTEN ABOUT SEASONAL, MODERN POLISH FOOD FOR MANY WELL-KNOWN MAGAZINES. DRAWING ON HER FAMILY HERITAGE, HER COOKERY BOOK WILD HONEY AND RYE: MODERN POLISH RECIPES WAS PUBLISHED IN THE UK AND AMERICA.

As a busy mother of three, Ren knows only too well the challenges of cooking family food when time is tight and inspiration is low. "Cooking has always been my favourite way of relaxing. Connecting with my readers, sharing recipes and helping them along with their food dilemmas is something that I will always enjoy."

Ren lives and works in Hertfordshire and when time allows, she holds supper clubs locally. She has hosted events at Tabure and at the Street Café in St Albans, as well as featuring on radio cookery segments such as on BBC Three Counties Weekend Kitchen and Radio Verulam's Community Kitchen.

Further afield, Ren has cooked at the River Cottage Festival and she has also been a judge for the Guild of Food Writers Awards. Her recipes have been featured nationally in Delicious magazine and in BBC Good Food Magazine and she has written for online publications such as Jamie Oliver.

com and The Guardian. Her recipes have even reached The National Post in Canada and Food 52 in the States.

Through her book, Ren succeeded in introducing a new audience to the modern and vibrant food scene in Poland today, with anecdotes from her trips to the breakfast markets of Warsaw, to stylish bars and vodka tours in Polish cities. Her Polish heritage recipes also bring a good dose of nostalgia to the table and often feature some of the Polish ingredients that have become more readily available in our shops now, such as alternative grains, pickles, ferments and preserves.

Ren loves to bake and her seasonally inspired tray bakes are her signature. Garden apples and Victoria plums often find their way into her recipes. Ren's baked cheesecakes have been a popular hit and you'll likely be served a Polish plum martini alongside your dessert at Ren's supper clubs, too.

POLISH MEATBALLS
WITH A FERMENTED CABBAGE SALAD

*Polish main meals are very often served with a raw vegetable salad on the side,
known as a surówka. It lightens things up, is excellent for gut health and provides
a nice contrast to the hot food it is served with. These meatballs are easy to make
for a family meal and can be made with turkey, pork or chicken mince. Potatoes
and carrots sprinkled with dill also go well here.*

FOR THE CABBAGE SALAD

*½ fresh white cabbage, very finely
shredded*

1 carrot, peeled

2-3 tbsp sauerkraut

2 tablespoons white wine vinegar

1 tsp sugar

2 tbsp vegetable oil

FOR THE MEATBALLS

500g turkey mince

2 shallots, very finely sliced

1 egg, lightly beaten

12 tbsp breadcrumbs

1 tsp dried parsley

Sea salt and black pepper

Vegetable oil

1 tsp butter

TO SERVE

*500g potatoes, peeled and soaked
in cold water*

500g carrots, peeled and chopped

1 tsp butter

5g fresh dill

FOR THE CABBAGE SALAD

Make the cabbage salad at least one day in advance. Save a few of the darker outer
leaves to garnish the salad. Finely shred the cabbage and one carrot (using a food
processor if you have one) and tip into a large bowl along with the sauerkraut.
Stir together the white wine vinegar, sugar, a pinch of salt and two tablespoons of
vegetable oil. Pour the mixture over the cabbage and stir well. Cover or transfer to
a lidded jar and keep in the fridge.

Preheat the oven to 200°c.

FOR THE MEATBALLS

Place the turkey mince, chopped shallots, beaten egg, four tablespoons of
breadcrumbs, the parsley and a good twist of sea salt and pepper into a large
bowl. Add four tablespoons of water and mix until just combined. Overmixing will
produce tough meatballs.

Wash your hands and shape the mixture into 12 small meatballs; they can either
be round or oval shaped. Sprinkle the remaining eight tablespoons of breadcrumbs
onto a plate and carefully roll each meatball in the breadcrumbs. Flatten them down
slightly with the palm of your hand so that they cook more evenly.

Pour a little vegetable oil into a large pan and add the teaspoon of butter. Pan-fry
the meatballs, first on one side until golden brown and then carefully flip them over.
You can do this in two batches. Carefully transfer the meatballs to an ovenproof
dish and finish cooking them for 10 to 12 minutes. Add 75ml of water to the dish
and cover with foil. Cook for 10 to 12 minutes.

Bring a large pan of salted water to the boil. Drain the peeled potatoes and cook
them for 10 minutes, or until soft.

Place the carrots into a separate pan and just cover with water. Add a sprinkle of
salt, sugar and a teaspoon of butter. Cook for 10 minutes or until soft, keeping an
eye on the water. Add a little more water if it evaporates down.

TO SERVE

Take the meatballs out of the oven and check they are cooked through. Drain the
potatoes and carrots. Serve with your pre-made cabbage salad, a sprinkle of fresh
dill and a drizzle of avocado oil, if liked.

Preparation time: 30 minutes, plus 1 day fermenting | Cooking time: 10 minutes | Serves 4

FROM FIELD TO FORK

ROTHAMSTED HAS BEEN AT THE CENTRE OF FOOD RESEARCH FOR YEARS, AND IS NOW ALSO A FANTASTIC PLACE TO EAT AND CELEBRATE IN THE COMMUNITY.

Anyone who knows Harpenden knows the world-leading Rothamsted Research Institute and beautiful Rothamsted Manor. Parts of the estate date back to 1212, and the Manor house and Conference Centre are home to events throughout the year, from cream teas on the lawn to weddings, birthday parties and other family occasions.

The Rothamsted Restaurant is a large, light-filled restaurant located in the modern conference centre building on the left as you enter the campus from Harpenden Road. Anyone is welcome to go in and make use of the restaurant, and the team of chefs, led by Jez Beasley, make delicious, fresh food, strong on eco-credentials. The menu changes with the seasons, so you might find a vegetable biryani, roasted butternut squash and coconut curry, aubergine parmigiana, smoked mackerel bubble and squeak or salmon teriyaki. You can also get a great sandwich, salad, bowl of soup or just pop in for a coffee and a cake. There is seating outside when the weather is kind, and the restaurant attracts lots of walkers from nearby Rothamsted Park, taking a break. There is lots of space inside for people wanting to hot-desk or co-work while enjoying a coffee or bite to eat, and hot-desking and WiFi is completely free. There's also ample free parking on site.

Rothamsted's commitment to the environment is evident; customers can take coffee grounds home for their garden. Where they can, they work with local suppliers, including Farr Brewery who make their own Rothamsted Beer (the hops come from wheat grown on site).

Rothamsted host many events throughout the year; afternoon teas take place in the Grade 1 listed Manor on various Sundays between May and September, and they hold cream teas in the summer as part of the national Heritage Open Days cultural festival. Film nights take place in the auditorium (they sell Darlish ice cream during the films, who are based at Rothamsted). Their seasonal gastro evenings will be launching in 2020 too.

Henry Dimbleby, co-founder of Leon and the Sustainable Restaurant Association, visited recently for part of his research into the new National Food Strategy. As Rothamsted are world-leaders in agricultural research and development there was plenty to talk about, and share with him.

At the heart of Harpenden for many years, Rothamsted is now using food to bring the community into its world.

PITHIVIER OF ROASTED VEGETABLES WITH ROASTED CAULIFLOWER

This light, fresh, vegan dish reminds our chef of his classic training and combines his vision for sustainability with his passion for food. Serve with a salad or seasonal, steamed vegetables such as peas and carrots (you can purée the vegetables if you want to be cheffy!).

FOR THE PITHIVIER

1 large roasted red pepper, skinned and deseeded

4 chestnut mushrooms, destalked and peeled

8 sliced circles of peeled butternut squash

4 sliced circles of aubergine

1 red onion, peeled and cut into rings

8 slices of courgette

1 tsp chopped garlic

½ tsp dried oregano

A sprig of thyme

Freshly ground black pepper and salt

1 tbsp olive oil

4 13cm x 13cm vegan puff pastry squares

Soya milk, for brushing

FOR THE ROAST CAULIFLOWER

1 large head of cauliflower, cut into about 12 florets

25ml olive oil

1 tsp curry powder

1 tsp turmeric

½ tsp sumac

10ml water

Preheat the oven to 180°c.

Cut the pepper into four circles using a 5cm ring cutter (all your vegetables need to be this size, or smaller). Place all the vegetables into a mixing bowl, add the garlic, oregano, thyme sprigs and oil along with seasoning, and mix.

Place the vegetables on a non-stick baking tray and roast for 10 minutes. Take out and allow to cool. Once cool, stack the vegetables alternately leaving the mushroom last to make four stacks then place in the freezer for 5 minutes to set the stack together.

Place each stack upside down on top of a square of puff pastry then carefully bring the corners of the pastry up to form a parcel that resembles a dome (if you like, place the pastry into a ladle before making the parcel to form a perfect dome). Seal the bottom and tidy up the bottom with some scissors. Turn each parcel the right way up and place on a baking tray. Gently score the dome and brush with soya milk. Turn up the oven to 190°c, then place the tray in the oven and bake the parcels for about 15 minutes until golden brown.

Meanwhile, make the roasted cauliflower. Place the florets onto a roasting tray. Mix the oil, spices and water and brush over the florets. Season. Cover with foil and bake for 10 minutes at 190°c (with the parcels is ideal). Take the foil off and cook for a further 10 minutes. Take out of the oven.

To build the dish, place a pithivier in the centre of each plate, and place the cauliflower florets alongside. Drizzle with good quality olive oil, if you like.

Preparation time: 15 minutes | Cooking time: 40 minutes | Serves 4

THE
BEST-KEPT
SECRET

MOVE OVER WILLY WONKA: HERTFORDSHIRE HAS ITS VERY OWN CHOCOLATE FACTORY, WHERE HIGHLY SKILLED CHOCOLATIERS MAKE DELICIOUS TRUFFLES, BARS, LOLLIES AND MICE READY TO SELL IN THEIR WELCOMING SHOP AND CAFÉ OR BE SENT OFF TO LONDON.

Tucked away in Woolmer Green is a real-life chocolate factory, where the Luder family and their talented team of 'truffletiers' use the finest Swiss chocolate to make their delicious range of chocolate bars, truffles and much more.

Brothers Peter and Hans Luder started making chocolate in the 60s, for many well-known London shops and restaurants (which remain a closely-guarded secret) and now daughters Nadine and Nina work alongside them, continuing the Lessiter's legacy which dates back to 1911. Throughout that time the focus has been on using only the very best cocoa and fresh ingredients for their chocolate. As Nadine explained: "the beans we use come from sustainable cocoa farms in the Ivory Coast and Ghana amongst others, and we use the Swiss method to take the chocolate from bean to bar. Our chocolate is conched for longer, so it still has the same distinctive, creamy taste it has always had. We only use fresh raspberry purée in our truffles and bars, for example, just as my father and uncle always did, as well as fresh cream from British farms."

Peter Luder trained in Switzerland as a chocolatier and as a patisserie chef (including at The Dorchester) – so he makes the dark, velvety sachertorte for sale in the café.

Inside the inspiring shop, tables and baskets are piled high with chocolate bars and boxes of truffles and there is something for everyone, from marc de champagne and salted caramel truffles to thick bars of finest dark chocolate, or perhaps a chocolate mouse or a bag of buttons? At Easter you will find rows of cheeky bunnies and ribbon-wrapped eggs, or you may prefer one of their famous classics, such as rose and violet creams, cherry brandies and mint thins. If you prefer to choose your own favourites, head to the counter and select your favourite chocolate and truffles to make your perfect box.

The homemade hot chocolate is a must-try in the newly expanded café. As Nadine explains, they use a traditional Swiss recipe using 72% dark chocolate so it isn't too sweet. You can buy pretty tins and bags of the drinking chocolate to take away. If you would like to learn how to make chocolate truffles and bars yourself, you can go along to a workshop, and of course, you get to eat it afterwards!

SERIOUSLY GROWN-UP HOT CHOCOLATE

*Forget your run-of-the-mill drinking chocolate, this is molten heaven. Using The
Secret Truffletier's luxurious drinking chocolate made from 72% cocoa flakes,
this hug in a mug tastes incredible on its own or if you really want to elevate it to
grown-up glory, add a shot of your favourite tipple.*

*250ml semi-skimmed milk (use whole
milk for decadence or oat/nut/coconut
milk to make this vegan)*

*4 generous tsp The Secret Truffletier 72%
cocoa chocolate flakes (or equivalent
good quality chocolate)*

1 tsp sugar (adjust to taste)

Optional:

Whipping cream and marshmallows

or

A shot of whisky, brandy or rum

Pour the milk into a saucepan and over medium heat bring to the boil, stirring gently
with a whisk to avoid burning the milk.

Turn the heat down so the milk is simmering and pour in the drinking chocolate
flakes and sugar.

Whisk vigorously and continuously until all chocolate has fully dissolved.

Pour into your favourite mug and, if using, add your spirit.

If desired, top with whipped cream, marshmallows and a sprinkle of chocolate
flakes.

Find your comfiest chair, relax and have a spoon handy for any excess melted
chocolate that you might find at the bottom of your mug. Enjoy!

Note: We have adapted our recipe for you to enjoy at home but to recreate our
signature frothy top, use half the quantity of milk to mix the chocolate and then top
up with steamed or frothed milk.

Preparation time: 15 minutes | Serves 1

BAKED TO PERFECTION

WITH 35 SHOPS AND COUNTING, SIMMONS IS SPREAD ALL OVER HERTFORDSHIRE LIKE THE STICKY ICING ON THEIR FAMOUS BELGIAN BUNS.

If you live or work in Hertfordshire, chances are you have bought a loaf of bread, cake, coffee, freshly made sandwich or a sausage roll from Simmons. Simmons have been baking since 1838, making it one of the longest running producers in our book.

The family-run business started with Eliza Simmons in the tiny hamlet of Roe Green, just outside Hatfield. Eliza's baking know-how was passed on through the generations and the descendants of the Simmons family still run the business today.

Simmons' bright and contemporary shops can be found across the whole of Herts including Hertford, Harpenden, Hitchin, Stevenage, Welwyn Garden City, Ware, St Albans and many of the hamlets and villages across the county, employing in excess of 400 local people.

The whole range of baked goods, both savoury and sweet, are still produced in Hatfield where the team work hard throughout the night mixing and baking then icing and decorating before delivering to the shops ready for the morning rush.

Simmons produce a range of artisan breads and cakes including sourdough, croissants, Danish pastries and jammy doughnuts as well as the famous hot cross buns (which are in demand all year round). Firm favourites include homemade carrot cake, lemon drizzle and sticky ginger as well as deep-filled bakewell tarts, cherry and almond and zesty lemon meringue pies. Gateaux, including the very popular rainbow cake, can also be ordered online ready to collect in any shop the next day.

Over the last few decades Simmons has also become associated with freshly produced coffees together with breakfast food to go such as breakfast baps and filled croissants. At lunch customers enjoy fresh sandwiches, baguettes and baps which are made fresh for every customer, including salmon, avocado and chicken. The fresh soups, such as tomato and basil or Thai vegetable and the vegan mushroom rolls are new favourites. As the day continues many come in for sweet treats such as brownies, thick chocolate caramel shortbread, sticky flapjacks and iced children's biscuits.

As a special treat, look for the Mill Green wholemeal loaf which is made from Mill Green flour, locally produced just outside Welwyn Garden City; surely a record for low food miles. Also did you know that Simmons have baked scones for Wimbledon tennis championships?

Simmons are a family baker who have continued to be successful by sticking to their values of using the very best ingredients to make products with love and pride. Long may the tradition continue!

CHOCOLATE CARAMEL SHORTBREAD

*We found it tricky to decide whether to include our recipe for sticky ginger cake,
or our rich chocolate brownies, but in the end it had to be our chocolate caramel
shortbread which always flies out of the shops. So here it is, to make at home!*

FOR THE SHORTBREAD

240g plain flour

160g butter, plus extra for greasing

80g caster sugar

Pinch of salt

FOR THE CARAMEL

125g butter

70g dark brown or muscovado sugar

70g golden syrup

390g (1 tin) condensed milk

TO FINISH

*200g good quality chocolate (we use
Belgian chocolate, milk, white or dark…
your choice!)*

Preheat the oven to 160°c. Grease a 15 by 25 cm (6 by 10 in) baking tin and line with greaseproof paper.

To make the shortbread, put the flour, butter and sugar and a pinch of salt in a bowl and rub together until thoroughly combined. Press into a dough then push in to the base of the tin. Flatten it, then prick all over with a fork. Put in the oven and bake for 30 minutes.

Meanwhile, make the caramel filling. Melt the butter in a non-stick saucepan, then add the sugar, stir well then bring to the boil and simmer for 5 minutes until dark golden brown. Add the syrup and condensed milk, stir, then bring to the boil and simmer for another 10 minutes. If using a thermometer, the temperature should reach 107°c. Stir regularly to avoid burning on the bottom.

When the shortbread is ready, carefully pour the caramel directly on to the shortbread base. Allow to cool until the caramel is set.

Melt the chocolate (you can do this in a microwave or in a bowl over a pan of boiling water) and pour over the set caramel. Allow to cool for 1 to 2 hours.

Remove from the tin and cut into 12 squares. Can be kept for up to 2 weeks in an airtight container.

Preparation time: 45 minutes | Cooking time: 30 minutes, plus cooling time | Makes 12

FARM TO FORK

KNOWN FOR THEIR DELICIOUS HOME-GROWN TOMATOES, PEPPERS AND AUBERGINES, SMALLFORD FARM SHOP AND GLASSHOUSE CAFÉ IS FILLED WITH THE VERY BEST PRODUCTS FROM ACROSS HERTFORDSHIRE.

Located on the site of a family-owned fresh produce nursery (Glinwell), Smallford Farm Shop and Glasshouse Café have been built from the history of the site; selling produce to local customers from pallets. You can now buy the delicious home-grown tomatoes, cucumbers, peppers and aubergines inside the modern, welcoming shop, alongside a wide range of local and independent products, creating a unique offering in Hertfordshire.

Look for the large greenhouses as you come into Smallford, nestled between Hatfield, St Albans and Colney Heath. There is plenty of parking and an easy way in for those needing wheelchair or pushchair access. When the weather allows there is a terrace with tables and umbrellas, and dogs are welcome with water bowls available. Inside is an array of Smallford's own vegetables along with award-winning farm meats, deli meats and cheeses, wine, beer, baked goods, and all sorts of daily groceries, luxury buys and gifts.

Co-owners Sam Cannatella and Joe Colletti have brought an incredible energy to Smallford Farm Shop, and the Glasshouse Café is a bustling place that brings people from miles away. Look for their own range of Cannatella & Colletti Sicilian sauces which uses their home-grown produce (very low food miles!) which you can buy to take home, and feature in dishes in the café.

In the shop you can find many Hertfordshire suppliers and artisan products. There is also a strong focus on vegan, vegetarian and gluten-free products, as well as sustainable packaging, like glass bottles for the fresh milk.

Local producers appear on the café menu too, including meats from Bridget B's and Harpenden company Twist Tea. The lasagne and penne pasta dishes are made with their own produce, of course, as are the salads and soups. Open from breakfast through to afternoon tea, you can get a great cooked breakfast and lunch includes salads, a daily soup, salt-beef and fish-finger sandwiches and burgers. Mouth-watering pastries, and cakes by Heaven Is A Cupcake are a great choice any time of the day.

Popular with locals, staff from the nearby University of Hertfordshire, cyclists, dog walkers, business professionals and families, Smallford Farm Shop has fast become a hub in the community.

SICILIAN ARANCINI

Sicilian Arancini, or rice balls, are one of the most recognised Sicilian foods throughout the world. These crisp, golden balls are typically served as a snack or street food throughout Sicily. Did you know that arancini means 'little oranges' in Italian? Delicious hot as a starter or for a main dish.

FOR THE RICE

1.5 litres chicken stock

1kg Arborio rice

2g saffron

300g Parmigiano cheese, grated

100g butter

FOR THE FILLING

2 tbsp olive oil

1 onion, finely chopped

1 carrot, finely chopped

1 celery stick, finely chopped

500g ground beef or pork

250ml red wine

300g tomato passata

2 bay leaves

150g frozen peas

Salt and pepper, to taste

FOR THE PANÉ (COATING)

3 large eggs, lightly beaten

600g breadcrumbs

TO COOK & SERVE

2 litres vegetable oil

250g mozzarella, broken into small pieces

Cannatella & Colletti arrabiata sauce, for dipping (optional)

FOR THE RICE

Bring the chicken stock to the boil and add the rice and saffron. Bring to a simmer and cook, covered, for about 20 minutes, until the stock is absorbed. Pour into a large shallow dish or pan and allow to cool. Once completely cooled, stir in the grated cheese and butter.

FOR THE FILLING

Meanwhile, to make the filling, put the olive oil, onion, carrot and celery in a large saucepan. Cook for about 10 minutes until softened. Add the meat and stir frequently until browned. Add the wine and cook for 1 minute until it evaporates. Pour in the passata, add the bay leaves, and bring to the boil. Lower the heat, cover loosely with the lid and simmer for 50 minutes until the sauce has thickened. Stir in the peas and cook for a further 10 minutes. Add salt and pepper to taste. Remove the bay leaves and set aside to cool.

FOR THE PANÉ (COATING)

To assemble the arancini, prepare two bowls with the beaten eggs in one and the breadcrumbs in the other.

Scoop a portion of the cooked rice into your hand and shape into a ball. Make an indentation in the centre with your thumb and add a small piece of mozzarella and one teaspoon of meat sauce. Close the rice mixture around the meat and shape into a ball.

Coat the ball in the egg and then roll in the breadcrumbs. Repeat until you have prepared all the arancini.

TO COOK & SERVE

Pour the vegetable oil into a deep, heavy-bottomed saucepan and place on a high heat. To test if your oil is hot enough place the handle of a wooden spoon in the pot and if the oil begins to bubble and fry around the handle, it is ready for your arancini.

Carefully lower in the arancini with a slotted spoon in batches of four until they are golden brown, about 3 to 4 minutes. Transfer to a dish lined with paper towels to absorb excess oil.

Serve the arancini hot with an arrabiata sauce for dunking.

Preparation time: 25 minutes | Cooking time: 1 hour 30 minutes | Makes 20-24 arancini

TREAT YOURSELF

WITH HER ON-THE-GO MEALS & INDULGENT PUDDINGS, TARA'S INNOVATIVE PLANT-BASED COOKING HAS TAKEN HERTS BY STORM.

Rainbow-coloured Vegan Treats might be a newcomer to the Herts food scene, but it has already made a huge impact in the county. You may have spotted the colourful pop-up kitchen at one of the markets around Herts and London. Often with a queue of hungry regulars. Tara prides the brand on being able to serve up unconventional vegan foods in a wholesome and tasty way, using original, cruelty-free recipes. Bestsellers Mac & Cheese, Meatless Meatballs and Warm Salted Caramel Pudding show that a vegan diet needn't mean you miss out on all the goodies!

Since beginning her street food venture at Camden Lock Market, Tara is now a regular at the St Albans charter market (Saturdays and Wednesdays) and Vegan Nights LDN in Brick Lane, has cooked for BBC Studio cafés as well as hosting supperclubs at local restaurants. Tara is behind the savoury menu at The Gin Cave and Bishop's Cave on Holywell Hill, as well as the dessert menu at The Odyssey Cinema, which includes her legendary Puddin' Pots in flavours that include Terry's Chocolate Orange, After Eight and Bounty. These delights make sure that dairy and egg-free customers don't miss out on being able to indulge.

Other ways to enjoy Vegan Treats are via home deliveries, weddings and corporate events. Tara also caters for Lush's annual Christmas party and has supplied treats for Sweaty Betty's 20th anniversary, Netflix film sets and made 1500 Puddin' Pots for clothing giant Asos. This January saw Vegan Treats go 'down under' as Tara supplied raw, sugar-free treats to health food stores surrounding Byron Bay, Melbourne and the Gold Coast

Over the last year, Vegan Treats has been shortlisted for Best Market Stall, Most Promising New Business and the Mayor's Pride Community Oriented Business of the Year award in St Albans, as well as being featured in various press outlets such as Vegan Living Magazine, The Herts Advertiser and BBC 3 Counties Radio. However, the most notable achievement so far has been Tara winning the prestigious Kate D'arcy customer service award at the Food & Drink Awards in September 2019, set in St Albans iconic town hall and filled with the city's most thriving local businesses for the evening. Tara was overwhelmed by the recognition she received and would love to maintain the momentum by opening a vegan restaurant in St Albans in the near future, with the aim of dismantling the stigma surrounding plant-based food and normalising a vegan lifestyle.

Photo: © Gizem Kumbaraci

PULLED JACKFRUIT TACOS

This tasty, plant-based twist on pulled pork will have the meatiest of guests satisfied! Loaded into crunchy corn tacos, topped with fresh colourful veg and lashings of garlic mayo, this allergen-free dish will cost you minimum effort, with maximum results.

2 x 400g tins of young green jackfruit, in brine, drained

2 red onions, peeled and sliced

2 peppers (any colour), sliced

2 cloves garlic, peeled and chopped

Rapeseed oil (or oil of your choice), for cooking

3 tbsp BBQ sauce (ensure no honey or anchovies)

2 tbsp Worcestershire sauce

1 tbsp dark brown sugar

1 tbsp smoked paprika

1 tsp cumin

1 tsp turmeric

½ tsp ground coriander

½ tsp ground nutmeg

½ tsp ground ginger

½ tsp ground cinnamon

Pinch of salt and pepper

TO SERVE

200g vegan mayonnaise

1 heaped tsp garlic paste

Pinch of dried herbs

3 spring onions, chopped

100g red cabbage, shredded

12 corn taco shells

1 lime, to squeeze over

Handful of fresh coriander, chopped

100g vegan cheese, grated (optional)

Break the jackfruit into shreds with your fingers or a fork.

Throw the onions, peppers and garlic into a preheated frying pan with a drizzle of oil and cook for 5 minutes.

Add the jackfruit shreds to the pan, adding a dash of hot water as you go, stir, then leave to simmer and infuse with the onion mixture for 10 minutes.

Add the BBQ sauce and all the spices, including the salt and pepper to the jackfruit. Stir, and then simmer for another 10 minutes, stirring frequently to ensure the seasoning has fully absorbed into the jackfruit.

Meanwhile, blend the mayo with the garlic paste and dried herbs and pour into a dressing bottle if you have one.

When ready to eat, pile the jackfruit mixture into the taco shells, topping with spring onion and red cabbage as you go. Garnish with fresh coriander, a squeeze of lime and lashings of your homemade garlic mayo. Add grated vegan cheese for good measure, if you like!

Preparation time: 15 minutes | Cooking time: 25 minutes | Makes 12 tacos, enough for 4 people

LOCAL LEGENDS

TRING HAS BEEN THE HOME OF THIS PROUDLY INDIE BREWING COMPANY,
KNOWN FOR THEIR QUIRKY BEER NAMES, FOR OVER 25 YEARS

Tring Brewery was established by Richard Shardlow in November 1992, taking its name from the East Hertfordshire town set in the Chilterns Hills, an Area of Outstanding Natural Beauty. The brewery launched with Ridgeway Bitter, the first in a range of cask ales using novel names and imagery to tell tales of folklore in the Chilterns. Richard comes from a family of brewers, affording him generations of knowledge to build a brewery in Tring, a town already steeped in beer heritage.

Richard was joined by fellow brewer Andrew Jackson (formerly of Whitbread) in 2000, the year the duo created 'Side Pocket for a Toad', the brewery's flagship beer. Today, the brewery produces an ensemble cast of traditional styles, complemented by progressive, innovative brews from Tring's new small-batch kit.

Premium malts and hops are blended with mineral-rich water from the Chiltern Hills, fermented with the brewery's signature yeast strain to produce beers of quality and character. Richard says "the team at Tring Brewery is proud of our rich history and independence; we believe these manifest in our award-winning beers."

The brewery is based on Dunsley Farm in Tring, just off the A41, minutes away from Tring Train Station, Ivinghoe Beacon and the town's branch of The Natural History Museum.

The on-site brewery shop offers draught and bottled beer to take away, along with local artisanal produce such as chocolate, biltong, chutneys and hot sauces. Tours are held every other Thursday night and Saturday afternoon, with a self-service tasting bar open on the weekend.

Tring Brewery has been awarded The Good Pub Guide 'Brewery Of The Year 2019', Chilterns Craft Beer Award 2018, Dacorum Environment Heroes 2019 and bronze in CAMRA's Champion Beer of Britain in 2016. Tring's award-winning beers can be found in pubs, restaurants and bars in the home counties, across London and beyond.

Special events at the brewery include beer and food pairings, heritage talks and Golden Toad Members' evenings; these are open nights with free-flowing beer and BBQ food, catering for a growing community of close to 800 loyal patrons.

STICKY DEATH OR GLORY RIBS WITH CHUNKY CHIPS AND CLASSIC COLESLAW

Now these are something else and with homemade coleslaw, they are a perfect sharing dish. Death or Glory is a barley wine, which means it has a residual sweetness, and it is this sugar content that provides the stickiness. This recipe is so easy and they can be prepared in advance. Feel free to make your own chips, however good oven chips will do the job.

FOR THE RIBS

Rack of pork ribs with a generous amount of the belly left on if possible (should only need 6-8 ribs if meaty!)

330ml bottle of Death or Glory Ale

250ml water

2 tbsp tomato ketchup

1 tbsp white wine vinegar

2 cloves garlic, peeled and very finely chopped

1 tsp Worcestershire sauce

½ tsp salt

1 green chilli, finely chopped

1 bay leaf

Freshly ground black pepper

FOR THE COLESLAW

3 tbsp good-quality mayonnaise

1 tbsp salad cream

½ tsp ground turmeric

Freshly ground black pepper

100g white cabbage, roughly sliced

25g mild onion, peeled and finely sliced

50g carrot, coarsely grated

1 medium hot red chilli, deseeded and sliced along the length

Preheat your oven to 180°c. Put all the ingredients (except for the ribs) in a high-sided baking tray. Stir well.

Place the tray on the hob and bring to a simmer. Place the ribs, meaty side down, into the tray, cover tightly with foil and place in the oven for 1 hour 30 minutes. Check every 30 minutes to make sure it is not cooking dry. If necessary, add a little boiling water.

After 1 hour 30 minutes the ribs should start to feel tender; if not put them back for a further 15 to 30 minutes. When ready, remove the ribs and place meat side up on a shallow baking tray and cover loosely with the foil. Increase the oven temperature to 200°c.

Pour the cooking pan juices through a fine sieve into a non-stick saucepan then bring to the boil. Continue boiling until the consistency is thick like syrup then, using a brush, coat the ribs with the sticky sauce. Place in the oven again for approximately 15 minutes until the edges of the ribs just start to blacken.

In the meantime, prepare the coleslaw by putting the mayonnaise, salad cream, turmeric and black pepper in a bowl. Give it a good mix and then add the cabbage, onion and carrot. Stir in the chilli to taste. Toss to combine.

Remove the meat from the oven and allow to rest for 5 minutes before serving.

Preparation time: 15 minutes | Cooking time: 1½ - 2 hours | Serves 2

A TASTE OF HISTORY

THE OLDEST PUB IN THE UK, AT THE HEART OF THE COMMUNITY, YE OLDE FIGHTING COCKS NEEDS VERY LITTLE INTRODUCTION.

Hertfordshire has some incredible pubs, with a strong brewing history, and talented chefs. But one stands out: Ye Olde Fighting Cocks is officially the oldest pub in the country (just check The Guinness Book of Records) with parts dating back to 793AD. A trip there today is stepping into history; the low ceilings, original beams, wonky walls and roaring fires remind you of all the people who have gone there before you, sheltering perhaps on a rainy day, or sharing stories of the working week. Yet this is not a pub stuck in the past; landlord Christo Tofali and team are forward-thinking and are at the very heart of the community, hosting events all year round, from films, to live music, comedy and beer festivals.

Ye Olde Fighting Cocks is in the most beautiful location, just a short walk from St Albans Cathedral and overlooking Verulamium lake. The large pub garden is bustling in the summer months, and there is often a barbecue (sometimes Christo's son is behind it!). Grab a table with lake views if you can.

On a chilly evening, grab a cosy spot near the real fire, and think of all those who have sat in the very same place before you!

Being an independent pub, Christo is able to choose an interesting selection of real ales, and has worked with local brewers Farr Brew to create his own beers including Black Listed. St Albans is the home of CAMRA (The Campaign for Real Ales) and they have held many events here, showing how good they think the beer is. Ye Olde Fighting Cocks has won the award for Best Pub in the St Albans Food & Drink Awards and CAMRA awards many times.

Food is at the heart of what they do, and the Sunday lunch is legendary, often serving over 200 people (you have to book). But the menu is always changing, to reflect the seasons and what the chefs fancy creating.

A natural publican, Christo takes the responsibility of protecting the legacy of this historic pub very seriously, while looking to its future. It is amazing to think that we can visit Ye Olde Fighting Cocks just as Oliver Cromwell did 400 years ago, while enjoying the very best of food and beer.

WINTER CHORIZO, CHILLI, PORK AND PULSE STEW

This is an easy one-pot dish which is completely amazing served with fresh bread and made with an ounce or two of love This always takes me a lot of time but it's worth every second. It has a chilli warmth and smooth velvety texture, with pork melting and the smokiness of chorizo rounding everything off. If you have any leftover take it to work the next day and it reheats wonderfully.

1 bottle good red wine (something oozing with berries and not too heavy)

Olive oil, for cooking

30g fresh root ginger, cut into 3 slices

6 green cardamon pods

150g chorizo, sliced about ½ cm thick

4 small hot chillies

750g shoulder of pork, cut into 4 cm cubes

200g flour (or enough to coat the pork)

1 large onion

6 large cloves of garlic, peeled

3 celery sticks

1 leek

1 carrot

1 red pepper

1 yellow pepper

1 large green chilli (medium heat)

2 large red chillies (medium heat)

1 tsp turmeric, heaped

1 tbsp tomato purée, heaped

2-3 litres vegetable stock

400g tinned whole peeled tomatoes

1 courgette, chopped roughly

400g tinned of butter beans, drained

400g tinned of chickpeas, drained

50g flat leaf parsley

50g fresh coriander

Sea salt

Cracked black pepper

TO SERVE

1 ripe lemon

300g natural yoghurt

Mango chutney

1 large fresh French stick

Preheat the oven to 180°c.

Add a few glugs of olive oil to a large steel, high-sided pot, put on a very low heat, then add the ginger, the 4 whole hot chillies, cardamom pods and the chorizo. Let this gently infuse in the oil while you start preparing the pork. Don't have the oil so hot that it fries the ingredients; be gentle and let it do its thing.

Season the pork with sea salt and plenty of cracked black pepper. Add to the flour in a large mixing bowl and coat the meat. Knock off any excess flour.

Remove the chorizo mixture from the pan and set aside, the oil left behind should have a red tinge and smell vibrant.

Turn up the heat and add the pork bit by bit so you keep the sizzle when you put it in the pan. Keep the heat up as we want the pork to fry and get a healthy brown colour. You may have to do this in two or three batches. Place the sealed pork into a bowl and set aside.

Cut the onion, garlic, peppers, celery, leek and carrots into medium dice. Put a hole in the remaining chillies with a pointed knife and add whole; fry them off on a medium to low heat in the same pan (you may need to add some more olive oil).

Put the vegetables in the pan and cook for about 5 minutes until they have a little colour, then add the chorizo mixture and stir in the turmeric.

Turn up the heat. Make a small well in the middle of the pan and add the tomato purée; stir for about a minute to release its oil and then stir in the vegetables, pork and all the juices.

Stir together and add a large glass of the red wine, maybe two.

Bring to a simmer and cook for about 5 minutes to reduce the wine. Add enough vegetable stock to cover well. Add the tinned tomatoes, stir, put on the lid and put in the oven for 2 hours. Check it from time to time, it will reduce but add more water if need be (you are going to need to dunk your crusty French stick in it later on).

Add the courgette, all the pulses and the chopped parsley, stir and return to the oven for another 30 minutes.

The stew is ready when the pork falls apart. Just before serving, squeeze over the lemon juice and serve with a dollop of yoghurt, some finely chopped chilli (no seeds), chopped coriander, and with a spoonful of mango chutney if you have some. Serve with a large French stick and butter in the middle of the table. Look out for the ginger and chillies; I like them but my wife doesn't; whether you eat them is up to you!

Preparation time: 15 minutes | Cooking time: approximately 3 hours | Serves: Feeds 6 generously

DIRECTORY

BATTLERS GREEN FARM SHOP

Battlers Green Farm
Common Lane
Radlett WD7 8PH
Telephone: 01923 856551
Website: www.battlersgreenfarm.co.uk

A farm shop based on the family farm with deli counter, fresh bread and cooked meals. The farm is also home to a café, independent butcher, fishmonger and greengrocer.

THE BEER SHOP

30-32 Hermitage Road
Hitchin SG5 1BY
Telephone: 01462 337440

71 London Road
St Albans AL1 1LN
Telephone: 01727 568030
Website: www.beershophq.uk

Tasting room and bottle shop featuring unusual, small-batch beers from the UK, Europe and the USA.

THE BISHOP'S CAVE

22 North Street
Bishop's Stortford CM23 2LW
Telephone: 07444 490634

19 Holywell Hill
St Albans AL1 1EZ
Telephone: 07458 930983
Website: www.thebishopscave.co.uk

Stylish wine bar and gin bar that also do cocktails and generous cheeseboards — you can also buy a great selection of wines, beers, gins and cheeses to take home.

BUONGIORNO ITALIA

66 Lattimore Road
St Albans AL1 3XR
Telephone: 01727 847673
Website: www.buongiornoitalia.co.uk

Treasure-trove deli packed with Italian foods, from panettone to pasta, as well as a great selection of British and European cheeses and hams.

CHARLIE'S COFFEE & COMPANY

87 London Road
St Albans AL1 1LN
Website: www.charliescoffeeandcompany.co.uk

Funky coffee van and coffee shop that attracts legions of regular customers for the delicious coffee, bakes and friendly vibe.

CHILLI BAR & KITCHEN

28/30 London Road
St Albans AL1 1NG
Telephone: 01727 840100
Website: www.chillibarkitchen.com

Stylish and delicious Indian cooking, with many favourites on the menu, alongside chef specials. This award-winning restaurant also has a funky bar for pre-dinner drinks.

CHILTERN OILS

The Moors
Wilstone Green
Wilstone
Tring HP23 4NT
Telephone: 01442 828478
Website: www.chilterncoldpressedrapeseedoil.co.uk

Award-winning cold-pressed rapeseed oil, grown and extracted on the farm and now sold to home cooks and chefs across the UK.

THE COBBLED KITCHEN

69 Harpenden Road
St Albans AL3 6BY
Telephone: 07812 599492
Website: www.thecobbledkitchen.co.uk

Cookery school that focuses on making cooking enjoyable and instinctive. Classes take place outside St Albans or at your home or chosen venue.

THE COURTYARD CAFÉ

11 Hatfield Road
St Albans AL1 3RR
Telephone: 01727 868877

Family-run café that focuses on delicious seasonal breakfasts and lunches with an ever-changing selection of home-baked cakes and bakes. You can also buy stylish homewares and art.

DIZZY BEE GRANOLA

For stockists go to www.dizzybeekitchen.co.uk

Delicious, small-batch granolas and bars made using only the very best ingredients. Available in shops and cafés all across Hertfordshire.

FARR BREW

7 The Courtyard
Samuels Farm
Coleman Green Lane
Wheathamstead AL4 8ER
Telephone: 07967 998820
Website: www.farrbrew.com

Thriving indie brewery with a tasting room as well as a growing stable of pubs across Hertfordshire.

THE READING ROOMS

36 The High St
St Albans AL4 8AA

THE RISING SUN

1 Front Street
Slip End LU1 4BP

THE RED COW

171 Westfield Rd
Harpenden AL5 4ND

THE EIGHT BELLS

2 Park St
Old Hatfield AL9 5AX

THE FLEETVILLE LARDER

129 Hatfield Road
St Albans AL1 4JS
Telephone: 01727 863237
Website: www.fleetvillelarder.com

Buzzing neighbourhood coffee shop with a wonderful selection of cheeses, along with shelves packed with groceries and things to go with your cheese!

GEORGE STREET CANTEEN

9a George Street
St Albans AL3 4ER
Telephone: 01727 831540
Website: www.georgestreetcanteen.co.uk

Busy family-run café that focuses on seasonal, home-made food, with wonderful views over St Albans cathedral.

HIBISCUS LILY

Letchworth Garden City
SG6 2TU
Telephone: 07807 592076
For stockists go to www.hibiscuslily.co.uk

Homemade chutneys, condiments, jams and marmalades with special flair. Everything is made with natural ingredients without the use of preservatives and additives.

LAURA KATE CAKE BOUTIQUE AND TEA PARLOUR

15 High Street
Welwyn AL6 9EE
Telephone: 07530 513466
Website: www.laura-kate.co.uk

Charming cake boutique and tea shop that specialises in afternoon teas and special occasion cakes. You can also just pop in for a cup of loose-leaf tea, served in pretty china cups.

LUSSMANNS

20a Leyton Road
Harpenden AL5 2HU
Telephone: 01582 965393
Website: www.lussmanns.com

"Everything a modern local restaurant should be", said Giles Coren about Lussmanns. These fish and grill restaurants have won many awards for the sustainable approach including using only MSC fish and many local suppliers.

LUSSMANNS

42 Fore Street
Hertford SG14 1BY
Telephone: 01992 505329

HITCHIN

25b-26 Sun Street
Hitchin SG5 1AH
Telephone: 01462 440089

TRING

21 High Street
Tring HP23 5AR
Telephone: 01442 502250

WAXHOUSE GATE

St Albans AL3 4EW
Telephone: 01727 851941

MCMULLENS BREWERY

26 Old Cross
Hertford SG14 1RD
Telephone: 01992 584911
Website: www.mcmullens.co.uk

Brewing in Hertford since 1827, McMullens now has pubs all across Hertfordshire and beyond, with pretty rural pubs and buzzing city centre pubs.

THE ORANGE TREE

166 West Road
Sawbridgeworth CM21 0BP
Telephone: 01279 722485

THE DUSTY MILLER

Burnt Mill Lane
Harlow CM20 2QS
Telephone: 01279 424180

PARKER & VINE

6B Leyton Road
Harpenden AL5 2TL
Telephone: 01582 712886
Website: www.parkerandvine.com

Head to Parker & Vine for delicious, fresh salads and imaginative bakes and cakes, as well as shelves lined with interesting deli foods. Take in your own cup for a great coffee to go.

PEARCE'S FARM SHOP AND CAFÉ

A10
Hamels Mead
Buntingford SG9 9ND
Telephone: 01920 821246
Website: www.pearcesfarmshop.com

Stylish café/restaurant and farm shop, with seasonal fruit and vegetables grown on the farm. You can also go for pick-your-own in the summer.

PER TUTTI

30 Holywell Hill
St Albans AL1 1BZ
Telephone: 01727 839991

PER TUTTI

222 High Street
Berkhamstead
HP4 1AG
Telephone: 01442 866400
Website: www.pertuttirestaurant.co.uk

Popular Italian restaurant that is always busy, with a focus on classic Italian food, from pizzas to pastas, grilled meats and fish.

THE PUDDING STOP

6 The Colonnade
Verulam Road
St Albans AL3 4DD
Telephone: 01727 830357
Website: www.thepuddingstop.com

Very popular café that sells mostly puddings! You can also spot the pudmobile outside St Albans train station and in St Albans city centre and at local festivals and events.

PUDDINGSTONE DISTILLERY

Unit 1 Artisan Workshop
Lower Icknield Way
Wilstone Green
Tring HP23 4NT
Telephone: 01442 502033
Website: www.puddingstonedistillery.com

Award-winning gin distillery that does tours, tasting workshops and cocktail making classes. You can buy the gins at the distillery or in shops, bars and restaurants all across Herts.

REN BEHAN

Website: www.renbehan.com

Author and ambassador for Polish food in the UK, Ren has also hosted pop-up suppers, showcasing the very best of modern, seasonal Polish food.

ROTHAMSTEAD MANOR

West Common
Harpenden AL5 2BG
Telephone: 01582 938500
Website: www.rothamsteadmanor.com

Leading the way in the UK's research into plant and food research and development, Rothamstead is also a fantastic venue for special occasions and events as well as home to a light, modern café/restaurant that specialises in seasonal cooking.

THE SECRET TRUFFLETIER

61 London Road
Woolmer Green
Knebworth SG3 6JE
Telephone: 01438 810990
Website: www.thesecrettruffletier.co.uk

Herts' very own chocolate factory, with a new shop and café. Still family-run, the creative and delicious chocolate uses only the very best beans, and they take them from bean to bar right here in Hertfordshire.

SIMMONS BAKERS

2 The Parade
St Albans Road East
Hatfield AL10 0EY
Website: www.simmonsbakers.com

With 35 shops and cafés throughout Hertfordshire, including Hatfield, Watford, Cuffley, Hitchin, Ware, Hertford, Hemel and St Albans you are never too far away from a delicious loaf of Simmons bread (or a doughnut!).

SMALLFORD FARM SHOP

Hatfield Road
St Albans AL4 0HE
Telephone: 01727 747340
Website: www.smallfordfarmshop.com

Glinwells has grown excellent tomatoes, peppers and aubergines for years and you can now buy them in the new farm shop, along with many local suppliers, and head to the café to try the Italian-inspired specials.

TARA'S VEGAN TREATS

Charter Market, St Albans
Social media: @tarasvegantreats

Tara and her street food stall have taken St Albans by storm and vegans and flexitarians head there for her delicious main courses and pud pots. Follow her on instagram for pop-ups and collaborations with other local businesses.

TRING BREWERY

Dunsley Farm
London Road
Tring HP23 6HA
Telephone: 01442 890721
Website: www.tringbrewery.co.uk

Tring is the home of this award-winning local brewery; the beers are named after many local locations and legends!

YE OLDE FIGHTING COCKS

16 Abbey Mill Lane
St Albans AL3 4HE
Telephone: 01727 869152
Website: www.yeoldefightingcocks.co.uk

The oldest pub in the UK, this charming and vibrant pub is also known for its great food, live music and involvement in many community events.